MW01491109

Laws of Life
in Agriculture

by Nicolaus Remer

Translated by K. Castelliz and B. Davies

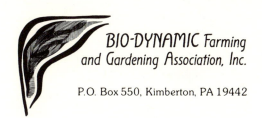

BIO-DYNAMIC Farming
and Gardening Association, Inc.

P.O. Box 550, Kimberton, PA 19442

Translated from "Leensgesetze im Landbau" published by
the Philosophisch-Anthroposophischer Verlag am
Goetheanum, Dornach, Switzerland, 1986.

This English edition published by the
Bio-Dynamic Farming and Gardening Assoc., Inc.
P.O. Box 550, Kimberton, PA 19442, U.S.A.
with kind permission of the original publishers.

Printed in the United States of America

ISBN 0-938250-40-X (softbound)

Contents

List of Illustrations

High quality food type   Roughage type
Negretti sheep   Indian mountain sheep

(Drawings by H. von Nathanius)

Photographs (following page 92)

Rye and vetches on drained marshland without manure

Manure treated with the bio-dynamic preparations has a particular effect on legumes

Rye and vetches on drained marshland with B.D. composted manure (10 tonnes per ha)

Shifting sand dunes as a result of neglected care of humus (Fürstenwalde, Spree)

Rich fungal growth on a manure heap treated with the combined preparation.

Soil profile of podsol with a hard pan. Bleached sand
horizon clearly visible below the top layer

Chromatograph comparison of carrot juice
(a) Juice from carrots sprayed several times with silica
    preparation 501, potentised to D7
(b) Juice from untreated carrots

Chromatograph comparison of red cabbage juice
(a) Juice from red cabbage sprayed several times with
    silica preparation 501, potentised to D7
(b) Juice from untreated red cabbage

Foreword for the English Translation of "Lebensgesetze. . ."

Twenty-five years ago the edition "Philosophisch-An-throposophischen Verlag am Goetheanum" in Dornach published Dr. Nicolaus Remer's "Leensgesetze im Land-bau", translated here and published as "Laws of Life in Agriculture". For 25 years many farmers in German speaking countries got inspiration and help for their work from this book. We can rightly call Nicolaus Remer a pioneer of the biodynamic movement. After graduating with a doctoral degree in agriculture and meeting the new biody-namic movement he worked for years on the first biody-namic research farm in Marienhohe near Berlin, Germany. He helped in the transition of big farms in the former east Germany which is now Poland. Widening his views was his agricultural work in wartime Ukraine.

What made his research so important for many farmers, medical doctors and scientists alike that we can be grateful for this English translation?

I had the privilege to observe and follow Nicolaus Re-mer's ways of working with farms and the research that resulted from it for 30 years. Over 500 monthly meetings of farmers of the region of North Germany took place between the beginning of his work there in 1949 and to-day, starting with about 30 people and growing to more than 200. Dr. Remer hardly ever missed a meeting and always made a presentation based on his research. Many of these meetings were accompanied by demonstrations in his vast research gardens located on a big biodynamic farm, gardens where he even now, being in his 80's, can create surprising phenomena in plant cultivation. He continues to inspire farmers with presentations out of his research based on the application of the ideas and advice Rudolf Steiner gave to practical farmers in 1924. His method is: To start on the side of the spirit, the idea, then to apply the idea in the practices of the farm, the garden, then to wait for the answer the farm, the field gives and eventually altering and amending the method of the application.

Nicolaus Remer has a unique way to bring the "spirit" into the daily activity on the farm, making the spirit or the idea the true means and motor of production. This "spirit" has to be on all levels practice—or it is not the true spirit but an abstraction. The practice of farming—in every detail—has to be permeated by the spirit. This principle led Nicolaus Remer in all his research and out of it he insisted that agricultural research has to be farm based and farm directed. The guide in it should not be scientific ambition but the needs of the farmers and the farms.

This concept radiates out of the essays given here.

Earlier than many others Nicolaus Remer understood that the downfall of agriculture, with its diminishing food quality and its negative impact on the environment, has to do with the social and socio-economic conditions of today's farming. He does not accept that a farm that produces out of the sustained fertility of the soil is similar to any other business. Farming becomes a business by producing substances from outside. If the farms are shaped into true harmonious organisms that individualize themselves more and more, which includes landscaping and the greatest possible diversity they can become the interest of everyone, not just the business interest of the farm family. Ways to shape the farm organism in this direction are given in this book.

Wilton, November 1992 Trauger Groh

Preface

The laws of life in agriculture propounded here have arisen from working with 30 farmers in this area of podsol soils in North West Germany. They were endeavouring to put into practice the ideas advanced by Rudolf Steiner in his course of lectures on agriculture given at Koberwitz in 1924. It is thanks to the courageous and tireless efforts of these farmers that, by carrying out these completely new suggestions, further results and a new understanding of life processes were obtained. The farms totalled about 1000 ha of agricultural land and produced for sale about 450 tonnes of grain, 800 tonnes of potatoes, 150 tonnes of field vegetables, one million litres of milk, 150 tonnes of meat and thus were not below the average yields in Western Germany. Production depended on natural manure produced on the farm. This was supplemented as far as possible by composted organic refuse and lime, combined with careful husbandry of humus.

According to the cultivations, manuring and crop rotations it gets, arable land oscillates between building up and breaking down, improvement and deterioration, between absorption and leaching out of nutrients. But even soils which, through climatic conditions are subject to leaching and degeneration as these podsols are, show a certain degree of productivity even in their yield of heath land herbage. Formerly sheep grazed these areas and their dung provided a constant source of nutrients for these poor soils. Some of the manure was used elsewhere in order to raise the productivity of other areas.

With animal manure the productivity of the soil, its active release of minerals and the biological breakdown of the subsoil was improved, thus benefiting the cultivated crops.

It was calculated (Hoppert, Limburgerhof, *Mitteilungen der deutschen landwirtschaftlichen Gesellschaft*, No. 31, 1959), that, mainly due to a higher stocking rate and better use of manure, the replacement of nutrients in these soils had so improved during the last hundred years, that an average increase of 800 kg to 1 tonne of grain per hectare was achieved. This means that, as a result of its own activity, more nutrients, e.g. 7 kg/ha potash and 8 kg/ha phosphates per year could be taken from the soil so long as no unforeseen circumstances occurred. Thus in most cases the farm was able to bear the loss of minerals represented by two tonnes of grain sold off the farm as cash crops, since the arable fields alternated between cash crops and fodder grown for the animals. There were however great differences between the different soil types. From this it can be seen that, to a certain extent, our soils could be made more productive in spite of the extraction of minerals from the underlying rock. This capacity can extend so as to affect both plants and animals. The process of gradual renewal is natural and was called "dynamic fertility" by the classical soil scientist Stebutt. When soil, plant-world and animal population blend into a higher organism, a harmonious, qualitative improvement in the food plants ensues.

We try to become more efficient by observing the laws of life and applying them. This results on the one hand in the promotion of soil fertility and on the other hand in paving the way towards achieving a nutritive quality in food the effect of which is visible in the health and performance of the livestock long before the produce finds its way to the customer.

Nicolaus Remer

Summary

During the 12 days of the course of lectures on agriculture given at Koberwitz in 1924,[1] Rudolf Steiner put forward practical ideas that even today are revolutionary for agriculture.

In order to maintain the original quality of food so that it remains real food, the following guide lines were laid down:

1. The manure requirements of the farm should as far as possible be produced by its own livestock.

2. Natural conditions which have been destroyed should be restored, e.g. the relationship between animals and hedges, bird protection and conifers, humus to enliven the soil, fungi on meadows within the framework of the landscape.

3. Rhythm and order in maintenance and care. Dynamic measures to control and direct the processes occurring in organic manure so as to stimulate the life processes of the plant.

4. Biological control of weeds and pests by means of new non-poisonous plant protection measures.

Much of all this still remains to be worked out.

The urgency in this century of finding a new way of husbanding humus in western agriculture as far as possible, has been recognised in manifestos, lectures and books by many leading personalities in science and agriculture, including Armand Denis, August Bier, Ernst

Hornsmann, Albert Howard, President Kennedy, Prince Bernhard of the Netherlands, Alwin Seifert, Guenther Schwab, St. Barbe-Baker, André Voisin, Ehrenfried Pfeiffer, Bernhard Grzimek.

Although today many people are concerned with the fate of the soil, there are few who will and can swim against the stream of a predominantly industrial development.

It is an urgent necessity to tackle the humus question in all countries in order to heal the destruction of the landscape and the drying up of the great continents. In the last 150 years, to the detriment of human nutrition, about 60% of the forests of the world, 60% of the wild animals and 60% of the humus reserves of the fertile areas of our planet have been destroyed.*

Large areas of our western European arable soils are over-used to the limit of their capacity, under the compulsion of economic competition. Nothing further can be gained by flogging them with synthetic nitrogen.

In the well-run farms of West Germany things have reached the point, according to the experts, "Where it is no longer economically possible to go on in this way. A new way must be found to ensure the economic survival of the farm".[2]

Care of the soil and manure is the first priority.

We integrate animal breeding into the landscape. We pay attention to home-grown fodder and the provision of hedges.

This way leads to the farm as a self-contained organism. In some circumstances a reduction in profits may ensue, which may be more difficult to overcome than on a conventional farm; but in the long run, life itself, fertility and

---

*These figures were quoted in 1968. Trans.

health improve only in the self-contained organic life cycle. This shows in good food utilisation, animal fertility, and in the quality of the milk and vegetables from farms that have chosen to take the step towards a self-contained status.

The regular use of herbal preparations advances the rotting process of animal manures and composts. These herbal preparations lead to the biological control of the soil life, thus leading the decomposition in the right direction, a prerequisite of modern humus management. In the living soil, fodder and food plants, cereals and vegetables develop harmoniously and achieve optimal quality.

The consumer appreciates this quality. He can sense how much care, work and human interest have gone into producing it. If he becomes interested he will collaborate and share in the responsibility for the fertility of the earth and for the future of mankind.

The whole farm individuality stands behind every single product. The basis for the whole soil life and fertility is the cow. In the life cycle of the farm the cow's digestion produces the manure which in its turn enlivens the soil for the benefit of the plant.

The herbal preparations control the fermentation of the compost, and a good compost is the basis of vegetable growing. The art of composting provides a product which has a hygienic effect on the soil.

The quality of the produce is an indication of the health of the farm. High fertility of the animals and healthy seed are the prerequisite for producing healthy food.

Chapter One

Humus in the Soil

For a long time it was not known what humus really was. It was thought to be rotted plants and remains of animal excrement which had simply decayed. This is not the case. Humus is an entirely new substance, the result of a hetero-polycondensation and oxidative polymerisation of a high-molecular compound[3]. It is a new combination, a newly built-up soil substance. Humus arises through organic substances being decomposed, transformed and newly rebuilt. The Russian soil scientist Vilyams says; humus arises mainly through the transformation of the excretions of soil organisms. The colour is partly due to certain soil fungi, algae and soil fauna. Not all combustible substances in peaty soils or even in the black earths are humus.

However, in the combustible substances in the black earths, there is a very high humus content, up to 90%. In peaty turf podsols there is usually not more than 50%, the rest being rotted, carbonised and peaty plant residues. This can easily be seen in these soils. Humus can therefore appear in very diverse forms. It was the Russian soil scientist Gedroits who discovered and recorded the difference and contrasting forms of humus at the turn of the century. He lived in Chernikov, north east of Kiev, almost at the dividing line between the soils with saturated and those with unsaturated humic acids. In the black earths of the steppes the humic acids are saturated with lime and other bases. The podsols begin in the northern wooded steppes and there the humic acids are unsaturated.

1

Saturated and unsaturated humic acids can be extracted from the soil by means of hydrochloric acid and ammonia. Soils with saturated humic acids are rich in nitrogen. Their humic acids contain up to 5% nitrogen and are highly saturated with lime, magnesium and potassium. They are able to dissolve silica and to form humus silicates[4].

Soils containing unsaturated humic acids are poor in nitrogen. Consequently podsols have a low nitrogen/carbon ratio. It can be as low as 1:40.

To alter the type of humus in the soil it is necessary to aim at a higher nitrogen/carbon ratio, i.e. the soil has to be enriched with protein. This has already been partially achieved on arable land treated according to our new method. In such soils the humus is different to what it was 10 years ago. Broadly speaking, the quantity is still the same but the quality is different: it is richer in nitrogen. This is proved by the yields. Where there is no change in the humus processes, however, the leaching of electrolytes continues and yields decline. The process of leaching can only be halted when the humic acids are base-saturated, and this has to start with manuring. It is difficult to achieve with sheep or pig manure. On light soils that have not been properly cultivated, sheep manure can produce the opposite of the desired effect. In a wrongly directed humus process it can result in raw humus, and the consequence is a bad product. The appearance of particular plants as weeds often indicates the type of humus present.

The flora of northern soils consists of dry "mineral plants" and woody plants such as pines, firs and heathland plants. The typical arable crop of the northern wooded landscape is rye, which has a high ratio of straw to grain. These soils have the tendency to form raw humus, which is inhabited by acid-forming soil fungi.

The more loamy soils of warmer regions have a high nitrogen-carbon ratio. Wheat, melons, cucumbers and fruit trees are grown there. If we go far enough south we find peaches, apricots and vines. Here flowering and fruiting processes predominate and the yield of honey is many times greater than in the north. All this is a reflection of the great contrasts in the humus processes, which can occur in innumerable stages.

As examples of the diverse humus requirements of plants we can take the garden strawberry and the rose. The strawberry is related to the potentillas and belongs to the Rosaceae. The garden strawberry is descended from the woodland or alpine strawberry, which is a plant of acid woodland soil and has an affinity to iron[5]. Iron, which we connect with the forces of Mars, supports fruit formation to such an extent that this can even take place in half shade. The woodland strawberry takes much iron from the soil, and thus a remedy can be made from it which promotes blood formation. The garden strawberry also benefits from iron. However, there is not much iron in garden humus, so in order to get its iron requirements it takes up a large amount of acidic humus substances.

With the rose it is different, although its red flowers indicate the Mars-iron process. The flower develops the inimitable attar of roses, or rose oil. For this it needs a rich alkaline manure, not an acid compost as does the garden strawberry. Roses can even be manured with oil. It can happen that some wild roses produce double flowers in one year and single flowers another year. This depends on the manure and on the development of a rich humus in the soil.

A distinction used to be made between rich and poor humus. Modern agrochemistry no longer does so. The strawberry and the rose show the difference. Today it is known that fat-like substances (i.e. those soluble in ether, such as fats and waxes) can be present in humus in some

3

quantity. They are also present in peaty soils. But these ether-soluble constituents are not necessarily found in rich humus. It is true fats, that are found in rich soils and these are mainly given off by the soil fauna.

Following our consideration of the influence of humus on the garden strawberry and the rose we can understand the cauliflower. Actually the cauliflower grows like a mushroom which is constantly seeking to become a flower. Mushrooms and trees are a complete contrast. The tree has its crown above the ground, the mushroom its "crown", or mycelium, under the ground. This inverted "crown" in the soil sometimes extends over several metres, as can be seen in fairy rings. What the tree does above the ground as regards nitrogen activity and the formation of protein, the mushroom does below the ground. Fungi in their thousands are at home in humus soils; the tree prefers more mineral soils. These soils cannot easily take in atmospheric nitrogen. It is mainly through their interaction, or symbiosis, with various fungi that trees absorb nitrogen.* The black-earth soils are enlivened by nitrogen and ensouled by the soil fauna. The world of the fungi develops underground like an inverted tree, and very quickly forms small fruiting bodies. The cauliflower is the "mushroom" among the brassicas. It wants to fruit very quickly. In order to support this tendency the plants need a manure comparable to the black earths, rich in nitrogen, with a high nitrogen/carbon ratio. This is why the cauliflower responds so readily to nitrogen. In more northern districts the requisite soil processes only occur after midsummer because only then is it warm enough.

---

*According to Professor Falck in *Die Bedeutung der Pilze fuer die Waldkultur* Sauerlaender Verlag, Aarau 1954, 75% of all trees are dependent on fungi. They penetrate the trees and serve them. A 40-year-old walnut tree with a normal nut yield produces 6 kg nitrogen which does not come from the soil. (Schanderl, *Bot. Bakteriologie*, Stuttgart 1946).

4

This is why in areas where it is difficult to grow cauliflowers, they should not be planted until after midsummer.

If we are to distinguish between different qualitative properties of humus we must observe how it tends to act on root formation, leaf growth or fruit formation.

For a plant there is always a "leap" from root, to leaf, to fruit. The soil also has to go through a corresponding development. There could for instance be raw humus in the soil, in which the plant finds it difficult to root. Since cauliflower does not easily grow strong roots, it will grow better in a mature nitrogenous soil. Rape and radish can develop roots in a poorer soil but the cauliflower must have a rich, mature soil. The various varieties of brassica have different needs.

With the cauliflower the fruiting process is emphasised, with rape the root development and with cabbage the leaf. The soil and manure should be prepared according to the varying needs of the plants. The first manurial requirement is that the plant can root quickly and well. The stage of decomposition of the dung is important. The nitrification process has to begin in the seed bed. Nitrites and nitrates have to be formed. During this phase the decomposing proteins need to be transformed into potassium nitrate (saltpetre). Nitrite and nitrate forming organisms initiate the maturing of the soil. Plant roots are dependent on the formation of potassium nitrate in the soil.

The next thing the plant needs for its leaf formation is carbon dioxide rising from the soil, which is also taken up by the surface roots.

For fruit formation, the plant requires nitrogen compounds such as those found in urine and poultry manure. One form of nitrogen found in poultry manure which has a strong manurial influence on fruiting is indole. At its various stages the plant needs different forms of nitrogen which can only be produced by soil organisms. If the soil

5

life cannot produce these, quality suffers. The activity of carbon dioxide from the soil is also made use of by the plant in different ways at various stages.

Roots need the process of nitrification in order to develop. In Spring our cereals depend upon this process.

Once they are flowering, plants no longer require potassium nitrate, but they need other compounds which occur in the soil. Among these are amino-acids, related to oestrogens, which should be present in the soil in very small quantities.

In vegetable growing the main emphasis is on leaf development which is dependent on carbon dioxide from the soil. Here the most important factor is the breakdown of cellulose which is done by quite different soil organisms. A whole team of organisms work at the breakdown and transformation of cellulose in the soil. This process can lead to a build-up of nitrogen in healthy soils.

The treatment of dung should aim at a rapid development of fungi, to avoid loss of ammonia. If they are to thrive, fungi (a kind of premature flowering process) need ammonia (NH_3) and its compounds, i.e. nitrogen in its reduced, not oxidised state. A high percentage of the nitrogen in fungi, sometimes up to 30%, is urea $CO(NH_2)_2$. In order that the beneficial fungi which cause breakdown can develop, sufficient air must be able to penetrate the fresh manure with mature compost in between. It would be best if the dung in the cow shed were already treated so that the fungi develop quickly once the heap is set up. In order to start off this process without too much work, a procedure involving the bio-dynamic "combined preparation" and a "parent compost heap", previously treated with the preparations, has been developed (as described in the next chapter). By encouraging fungal proliferation and fermentation in this way, saturated humic acids will develop in the manure. Later some dolomite (magnesian limestone) or marl (argillacious calcium carbonate) can be incorporated to help it along.

It is interesting that the whole process of decomposition does not begin with the formation of potassium nitrate which is what the root needs. Compared with the plant, the process of decomposition runs in the opposite direction, i.e. from the flowering process (fungal development) via cellulose breakdown with the accompanying formation of carbon dioxide for the leaves, to the formation of potassium nitrate required by the root.

Apart from this general treatment of manure, a special compost for the Leguminosae is recommended. This compost should activate the nitrogen-fixing bacteria when they are separated from this host plant. In this phase the *Azotobacter* bacteria behave like "plant-animals" and become more active. When they find new host plants they can now accomplish more. To make this compost for legumes, clover-turf and such like should be inter-layered with the manure. To get a neutral compost it is advisable to include some dolomite (magnesian limestone). This compost, containing rhizobial bacteria, is a way of increasing nitrogen in the soil. It is of particular benefit to legumes if the use of the compost goes hand in hand with deep aeration of the soil.

For manuring grassland and pasture large quantities of compost materials are needed because the supply of nitrogen from dung is less important than stimulating plants and soil. They will then avail themselves of the nitrogen from the air. If grassland is treated like arable land, cows are likely to get milk fever and grass tetany (grass staggers). This can be brought about by too much organic manuring as well as by mineral fertilisers.

For grasses it is necessary to activate their assimilation, which leads to an increase in dry matter. André Voisin has pointed out that it makes a great difference to animals

7

whether grass contains 15% or 30% of dry matter. With 30% dry matter, cattle need less than half of the quantity of fodder. A higher dry matter content and well developed protein are not achieved by lavish mineral fertilizer or un-rotted organic manure, but by compost. Compost combined the organic substances with silica. It also helps the atmospheric nitrogen to find its way into the sward. It supports the development of nitrogen-fixing organisms, both those which are attached to the roots of legumes and those which are living free in the soil.

As well as correct manuring, pastures also require correct management. If you overgaze in Spring when there is but little growth, there will be a great increase in white clover. The grasses will diminish. The highest yield is obtained when the grasses constitute 80% of the herbage. Correct control of grazing increases the proportion of grass and therefore the feeding value.

Thus a farm needs three different types of solid manure:

(a) basic manuring with properly treated dung

(b) leguminous compost

(c) the bulky mixed "earthy" compost for grassland and pastures.

Even if it is not possible to do all this immediately, it should definitely be the ultimate aim.

Because northern soils do not contain sufficient humus to initiate the necessary nitrogen processes, they must be assisted with top dressing. For this fourth type of manuring, solid as well as liquid manure can be used, but it should be highly concentrated. In the case of solid top dressing the water content should be reduced by careful composting. In order to keep the carbon/nitrogen ratio high it is good to mix dry poultry manure into the composted manure. The incorporation of protein-rich material such as hair, skin, wool, feathers or bristles, after a short period of fermentation, makes the manure more potent. Care must be taken that the decomposing protein substances do not reach too early the stage they should only develop when in the soil.

These observations make it evident that it would be desirable to have a detailed manuring plan and prepare the various composts and manures for each field so that the humus can be build up. Planned manuring helps to save manure.

Everywhere in life there are simultaneous processes of building up and breaking down. Decomposition can predominate, but if humus is to be increased, the building up process must be the stronger. When grassland gets the right compost at the right time, the humus increases. If, for instance, pigs are kept on a farm with a fish (carp) pond and the pig manure is cast into the pond, the carp will have extra food and sludge will be formed at the bottom of the pond. When the carp are fully grown, they are taken out, the water is let out and the sludge, which is far richer than the original pig manure, can be composted and spread over a larger area than the pure pig manure would have served. Other such ways of augmenting the supply of manure can be devised.

On "Klein-Südstedt" farm the constituents of a sandy field were analysed regularly. Initially the field had 0.06% nitrogen in the top 10 cm of soil and 1% humus. It was a very difficult field, but gradually the nitrogen increased to 0.09%.

Crimson clover and grass was sown as a catch crop. Part of it was manured in Autumn with rotted manure, the other part in Spring. The potatoes which followed showed a marked difference in favour of the autumn manuring. It must be realised that grass roots grow strongly between October and May, so long as the soil temperature does not fall below 5°C. As a result of the autumn manuring, root growth is stimulated and the growing period is prolonged due to the protection from frost afforded by the soil cover. This encourages the development of humus. The grasses are the greatest helpers. On podsols, red fescue and smooth meadow grass can be sown because their roots penetrate up to 35 cm if the pH value is 6.3 to 6.5. On wet soils with a pH of 5.5 this is not possible. There Yorkshire fog thrives which only penetrates to 10 cm.

In the meadows of northern Germany rough meadow grass predominates, because the soils are acid. Rough meadow grass is an entirely different grass from smooth meadow grass which is an outstanding fodder grass and spreads by runners. In order to encourage smooth meadow grass the pH value should be raised by composting. Lime should be added to the compost heap. Where smooth meadow grass thrives, conditions are also congenial for other good grasses like red fescue, timothy and ryegrass. Smooth oatgrass is found in deep soils and meadow foxtail in wet meadows. Their root systems will spread to a depth of 35 cm. By composting and raising the pH value, soil depth gradually increases.

Another way of raising the nitrogen content of the soil is by means of legumes. In a field of lucerne the humus content in the top 10 cm of soil was raised by 0.5% by the combined effects of compost and lucerne. The upper 10 cm of one hectare of arable land consists of 1500 tonnes of soil. An increase of 0.5% therefore means 7.5 tonnes of humus per hectare. In the garden an increase of this order can be achieved by a 1 cm dressing of compost.

On arable fields the building-up of humus is usually very slow, but its breakdown or decomposition is very rapid. If the humus content of the soil has been increased by 0.5% after three rotations, something has really been accomplished, and it represents an increase in capital that does not appear in the balance sheet. It is part and parcel of agriculture to build up the soil and raise its fertility to counteract the continual loss.

Chapter Two

Controlled Decomposition of Manure by Means of the Bio-Dynamic Herbal Preparations

Development of the Combined Preparation

In 1941 attempts were made to find tests of the effectiveness of the bio-dynamic herbal preparations made from yarrow, chamomile, nettle, oak bark, dandelion and valerian as described in the *Agriculture* course. A simple test was devised in which the preparations were used as seed baths. The individual preparations were placed in glasses filled with one litre of rainwater and stirred for 5 minutes. Seeds of peas, beetroot, spinach, tomatoes, cress and radishes were immersed for 1 hour. The effect of this treatment was visible in the different growth of the plants and was characteristic for the individual preparation plants. Chamomile was particularly favourable for peas. Tomatoes and spinach responded best to nettle. The other plants also showed their effects. These results were subsequently confirmed by the late Martha Künzel, who ran similar trials.

The next test was to confirm the phenomenon whereby nitrogen is increased in the yarrow and chamomile preparations. The nitrogen content of dried yarrow was ascertained. Then the yarrow preparation (502) made from the dried herb was tested. There was an astonishing increase of nitrogen. But if the preparation was not carefully made,

13

there was no increase. Numerous analyses have confirmed this.

The nitrogen content of 100 g of dried yarrow is from 1.5% to 1.8%. In the finished preparation the nitrogen content was from 3.5% to 3.7% if the preparation was well made. Thus, in spite of losses due to breakdown, there was increase of nitrogen of between 1.5 to 2.0 g in some cases. When nitrogen increases in the course of the normal rotting process, 50 g of carbon are consumed for every gram of nitrogen. Nitrogen-fixing micro-organisms get the energy they need for the fixation of atmospheric nitrogen by converting carbon to carbon dioxide. But the 100 g of yarrow contains 55 g of carbon. Thus more than the entire yarrow would have to be used and decomposed to enable such an increase to occur. But this is by no means what happens. The increase in nitrogen is not of a kind normally known in biology. Here we are faced with an entirely new kind of biological increase of nitrogen. It is a process which is not even possible with sugar. When fields are manured with sugar (molasses) it is possible to produce an increase in nitrogen. The amount of carbon required for the biological fixation of 1 g of nitrogen would be 25 g in the case of sugar. But there is no sugar in yarrow. Carbon is present mainly in the form of cellulose and the like. This proves chemically what was stated in the *Agriculture* course in 1924, namely that we have here a completely new form of nitrogen production.

These investigations were further extended to ash analyses of plants. Innumerable tests were made with the yarrow and chamomile preparations. The indisputable result was that here we have an astonishing biological fixation of nitrogen; provided that is, the preparations have been well made and not been spoilt or gone bad in any way.

Experiments in 1957	
Dried yarrow flowers	1.54% nitrogen
As preparation made near Peine	2.66% nitrogen
As preparation made near Bremen	2.31% nitrogen
As preparation (compacted)	2.46% nitrogen
As preparation (loose)	3.73% nitrogen
Dried chamomile flowers	2.70% nitrogen
As preparation (compacted)	2.70% nitrogen
As preparation (loose)	3.62% nitrogen

The increase in nitrogen can be attributed in part to the loss of weight during decomposition, but with yarrow the increase was repeatedly so great—more than twice the original quantity—that we must assume that nitrogen is actually produced by living organisms and substances. The potassium in the ash decreased from 30–31% to 5–6%.

The other preparations have different properties. Nettles ensure that the ratio remains constant, that there is no loss of nitrogen. Oak bark and dandelion are important for other processes.

The synthesis of nitrogen by yarrow can be scientifically established. This fact was pointed out by Rudolf Steiner in 1924 from a different perspective. A fact worth recording.

A phenomenon that particularly impressed E. Pfeiffer was that the activity of certain soil organisms was stimulated by the preparations, amongst others the microbial organisms particularly prevalent in the black earths. To these belong the streptomycetes, then already well known. Waksman, who discovered various antibiotic substances in the streptomycetes, observed that a great many of these substances appear in the black earths and have the effect of purifying the soil and ridding it of pathogenic organisms. Through these fungi soil nutrients become available to the plant roots[6]. They regulate humus formation in the soil and inhibit putrefaction. The development of the streptomycetes can be stimulated by the bio-dynamic preparations. Indeed, it proved possible to affect the activity of a great variety of organisms controlling the decomposition of organic material. It was found that micro-organisms, for the most part, can alter their characteristics[7]. With larger organisms changes are more difficult. Yet, a hundred years ago, cows weighed only half as much as they do today. Their milk yield and butterfat have also increased. Thus it is also possible to produce changes in larger organisms. The possibilities are much greater, however, with micro-organisms. This is made use of in medicine, in protective inoculation against virulent bacteria. In a similar way the life processes in compost and manure are activated by treatment with the above-mentioned herbs.

The observations of E. Pfeiffer were very important and led to new practices in municipal composting. Pfeiffer worked especially on municipal organic refuse, knowing that in the future it would not be possible adequately to manure agricultural land organically from its own resources, because during the last 100 years the soil has suffered such destruction of humus. The added organic fertiliser must be properly prepared and pre-digested so that it can be incorporated into the living soil without harming the soil organisms, and in such a form that the agricultural organism can utilise it.

The treatment of cow dung was often a problem. By continual monitoring of the nitrogen and humus content new methods were developed. The heating up of the manure had been found to lead to great losses of nitrogen, which were also incurred by putrefaction due to constant wetness. In treating cow dung it was necessary not only to attend to these technical problems but also to take advantage of the preparations as described by Rudolf Steiner in order to make better use of the cow manure than we had done hitherto. It was important to control the breakdown and transformation of the dung from the earliest stages. Decomposition had to be balanced by an appropriate synthesis. The best and most practical way of incorporating the herbal preparations in the dung had to be found. What we did was to make a "combined preparation" of all of them together, as was done earlier with the so-called birch pit manure.* The difficulty was to make a preparation that kept well and was dry and easy to use, and could be used in the cowshed or outside. It took seven years' work to try out various ways of making and using this preparation and observe its effectiveness.

By using the combined preparation it was possible to start treating the manure in the cowshed, as it was produced. It was always noticeable how the smell changed at once. The effect of the combined preparation could also be observed in deep litter yards. In comparing the manure heaps built subsequently from manure treated thus with the combined preparation and those left untreated, it was found that with this early treatment soil fungi developed more quickly and 10–15% of the usual nitrogen loss could be avoided.

The heaps are set up as follows. With fresh refuse and fresh dung it is better to begin by building a layer about 40 cm high for better aeration. It should be watered with a solution of the combined preparations and then covered. After 14 to 20 days it is built up as a compost heap to a height of 1.5 m and further treated with the bio-dynamic herbal preparations. After six to eight weeks, breakdown and transformation are generally so far advanced that it can be used.

One head of adult cattle normally produces 10 tonnes of dung per year for the farm. Of these 10 tonnes, about

* And more recently, the cowpat pit. (transl.)

2 tonnes are dry matter. Normal stocking rate should be at least 1 head of adult cattle per hectare of agricultural land. Ideally it should be 1.2 to 1.4 head per hectare. This would make it easier to be self-sufficient in manure. If the method of starting and building up the heap with the combined preparation as described above has been followed, the 2 tonnes of dry matter will often contain 2% of nitrogen as against 0.7-0.8% formerly. In 2 tonnes of dry matter this 2% amounts to 40 kg of nitrogen. Of these 40 kg, 80% was formerly lost. There is no doubt that through treatment of this sort, 15% of the nitrogen loss can be saved and that the nitrogen in the manure is in a better form. A saving of 10 to 15% represents 4–6 kg of nitrogen per hectare.

It follows that use of the combined preparation is worthwhile. We have here a visible and demonstrable result of a controlled and guided fermentation in the dung, stimulated by an ammonia-consuming, fungal rotting process.

Of course this by no means solves the nitrogen problem of a farm, for with intensive cropping, not 6 kg, but at least 60 kg/ha of nitrogen is required. But one should be thankful for this to start with. However, the missing 54 kg/ha of nitrogen will have to be supplied by liquid manure and other means. Besides this, the in-breathing of nitrogen into the soil by means of legumes must be encouraged. These nitrogen gatherers are symbiotic plants. They coexist with micro-organisms of the *Rhizobium* genus, and with the bacterium *Azotobacter*. There are nine sub-species. These organisms go through a free-living stage, when they are not attached to a plant root. In this state they do not take up nitrogen but are just like small animals which eat. They are then no longer little nodules but become somewhat elongated and develop little "arms" with which they can propel themselves about in the damp soil. During this time they are refreshing themselves. This life-cycle was not known previously. Research, especially in Italy[8], has shown that radicicolous bacteria are weakened by the vitamin C content in the greenplant. In their free-living stage the bacteria are like rudiments from a primeval time, when as yet light played no part. They really become "plant-animals". When, after this condition, they return to the plant roots, they can now work harder. It goes without saying that by means of treated manure and compost these organisms become much more active. It has always been found that after this treatment legumes grow better. This is even the case on drained marsh soils which definitely do not have the pH value required for growing legumes. The performance of legumes can vary greatly. It used to be assumed that legumes only took up nitrogen from the air for their own use. But the Nobel prizewinner Virtanen established the fact that legumes also give off nitrogen compounds into the soil, that they excrete amino-acids. These excretions were demonstrated in clay soils. He identified amino-acids which were excreted by the legumes and directly taken up again by other plants.

Higher plants are able to take up amino-acids directly. When such nitrogen compounds are available to them they make better use of them than they would of nitrogen in the form of ammonia or potassium nitrate.

The fungal organisms which develop a rapid growth in the soil do not live in sunlight. In contrast, the higher plants have roots and prefer potassium nitrate and other forms of nitrogen. But the higher plants produce ammonia in their flowers. If you pile apple or pear blossoms on a heap, they give off a smell like herrings, owing to the ammonia derivative trimethylamine. In the flower the plant has a relationship with ammonia, in the root with potassium nitrate.

The consumption of ammonia is, for us, a very advantageous activity of these small fungi. The early development

Soil nitrogen before and after a legume crop, with biological pre-treatment of the soil

Place	Crop	Soil type	Nitrogen content of the top 10 cm of soil, in %	
			Spring	Autumn
Observations in 1956				
Nordenham	beans	clay	0.26	0.46
Klein-S.	mixture	sand	0.09	0.10
Lil.t.	Peluschken (field peas)	drained peat-land	0.38	0.42
Wö.	serradella	sand	0.07	0.10
Observations in 1957				
H. Wald	beans	clay	0.14	0.18
Olbg.	beans	reclaimed coastal marsh	0.20	0.23
Strö.	mixture	sand	0.14	0.18
Fuhlh.	beans	loam on slope	0.09	0.13
Beven.	lupins	sand	0.08	0.09
Hasenm.	lupins	sand	0.09	0.13
Lil.t.	vetches	drained peat-land	0.78	0.92
Bolting	clover	humus sand	0.25	0.30

of fungi in manure must therefore be encouraged. The ammonia formed by the decomposition of protein, and especially the breakdown of urine, is taken up by them. The breakdown if urine cannot be prevented as it is caused by urease, an enzyme requiring a high pH value, and having a unitary configuration. Other enzymes consist of both an enzyme and a co-enzyme. In dung, nitrogen compounds are broken down by decomposition, ammonia is produced and escapes. The fungi can take up this ammonia. They also develop antibiotic substances, fungal acids such as penicillin for instance which inhibit putrefaction. When making the combined preparation this development is continued in the manure. The ammonia is fixed and putrefaction is prevented. This explains the higher nitrogen content of prepared manure.

In order to have a continuous check of the effectiveness of the combined preparation, a trial involving pigs was set up in 1964, which is described in more detail in the next chapter.

Because the pig likes humus and searches out fungi, it was the obvious animal to choose. It consumes five to six times as much protein as does man and is therefore in great danger of processes of putrefaction in its intestines. Toxic substances arise in the intestines, which are a burden to the organism. To counteract this, pigs seek the antibiotic effects of humus.

There was clear evidence from the analysis of the urine and the weight gain that the combined preparation guided the fermentation processes in the pigs' intestines in the right way, as it does in manure and compost heaps.

In 1965, the seventh year of the work, the question arose as to the content of the important vitamin B in the combined preparation. Soil contains a great number of vitamins and it is known today that they are very important for the higher plants. Five or six vitamins are known which are taken up by plants and which promote growth when the plant finds them in a living soil. Vitamin B_{12}, cyanocobolamin, is an especially important one, well known for the treatment of anaemia. Research has shown that the human and animal organism can itself produce vitamin B_{12}. There is a fundamental difference between plant and animal proteins in their vitamin B_{12} content. In plant protein only traces are present.

Extensive research has been done on the vitamin B_{12} content of foodstuffs. Oysters, for instance, are very rich in vitamin B_{12}, fish less so. It varies greatly in different animals.

The cow is a champion producer of vitamin B_{12}. She is

also a champion in synthesising protein, and vitamin B_{12} is necessary for this. Good utilisation of fodder requires vitamin B_{12}. Without it, the metabolism suffers. The cow lives in symbiosis with micro-organisms in the rumen where vitamin B_{12} is produced, and it is there that the synthesis of protein begins. Ammonia arises at the same time. Part of this passes to the liver and is transformed into urea. Bovine liver contains 0.06 mg of vitamin B_{12} per 100 g of substance, pig liver only 0.04 mg. The pig kidney contains 0.015 mg. In the meat the content is considerably less—only 0.001 mg.

Protein utilisation by cattle from roughage is 1:2 as against 1:4 by pigs. This food conversion is probably connected with vitamin B_{12}.

As we have seen, vitamin B_{12} is generally only present in traces. The tests are very complicated. An extract has to be made and the vitamin B_{12} content determined by means of micro-organisms (e.g. *Poteriochromonas stipitata*).

The combined preparation was tested in the Swiss Vitamin Institute in Basle by this method, using *Poteriochromonas stipitata*. A content of 0.010 to 0.011 mg per 100 g was established in a one-year-old sample. This was the same amount as was found in cattle or pigs' kidneys. The daily human requirement is 0.014 mg of vitamin B_{12}, though we can also produce it in our own organism.

The sample tested was of the dry preparation. It should be realised, however, that this vitamin B_{12} content is due to a process involving micro-organisms. With the combined preparation we can control the process. Here we have found one piece of the puzzle regarding the indication given in passing by Rudolf Steiner, that the nitrogen problem will be solved in this way.

Before the war, Schanderl[9] of Geisenheim had found that many plants were able to extract nitrogen from the air. In 1963 a paper appeared in Switzerland[10] in which it was established chemically, not bacteriologically, that plants not in symbiosis with nitrogen-fixing organisms, i.e. non-legumes, were able to extract nitrogen from the air. What is interesting in this work is that maize was used for the experiments as well as sterile peas. Now maize is an extremely nitrogen-hungry plant, but it was shown that it can extract 40% of its nitrogen requirements from the air if there is sufficient vitamin B_{12} in the region of its roots. This work demonstrates that, with the new manuring methods instigated by Rudolf Steiner, the whole nitrogen question appears in another light.

A 10 to 15% saving of nitrogen by preventing the loss mentioned earlier, is something that can be done on many farms, and it should be possible to extend this further. But it must be emphasized that it is also very important to treat the manure heap with the individual bio-dynamic preparations as well, as is described in the *Agriculture* course of 1924. The combined preparation, as has been shown, is convenient and effective for getting the preparations into the fresh dung as early as possible. It is important to find the dynamic possibilities of this new kind of manuring.

Nevertheless, these things, although appearing scientifically so well demonstrated now after 7 years of work, need to be developed much further. They have a still deeper background.

To achieve a manuring which will maintain the humus level in the soil and improve it as much as possible, well rotted manure is better than fresh manure or liquid manure[10].

The effectiveness of manure can be enhanced through treatment in progressive stages. The aim is the rapid development of fungi under aerobic conditions at a temperature of about 35°C (25–50°). The manure is then piled up with soil and other materials in larger heaps. This rotting and the resulting crumbly structure of the manure is especially important for sandy soils. At this later stage are added the individual herbal preparations of yarrow, chamomile, nettle, oak bark, dandelion and valerian to control and direct the processes of transformation.

Chapter Three

Effect of the Combined Herbal Preparation on Fermentation Processes

For the regulation of the fermentation processes in farm-yard manure, use is made primarily of compost preparations made from the medicinal herbs as mentioned earlier. They are added as supplements in minute quantities.

Owing to the great variability of the fermentation process in organic refuse, there are methodological difficulties in obtaining quantifiable results from bacteriological tests of treatments with these supplements. A chemical procedure has therefore been sought. Following preliminary microchemical investigations on plant extracts and human and animal urine, a test method involving supplementary feeding of pigs was adopted.

The pig is an effective processor of protein. Compared with the human being it can consume far more protein without ill effects, although even the domestic pig is of course also liable to metabolic disorders when given excess protein. At a live weight of 60 kg. a pig will eat 265 g. of protein, or 3–4 times the human norm. The biological regulation of the intestinal fermentation processes is therefore of great importance in the pig, and it is for this reason that it so readily consumes certain humus components. The daily course of the digestive processes can be followed in the urine. This is also true of human urine, as preliminary studies of hundreds of samples have shown. It was thought likely that giving the above-mentioned combined herbal preparation as a feed supplement to pigs, even in minute quantities (1 g. per animal per day, the content in the preparation being 10%), would have an effect on the urine and its chemical composition. It was possible to demonstrate qualitative differences in milk by means of urinary analysis of young pigs still being fed exclusively on milk[11].

In a feeding test with 18 young pigs having an average initial live weight of 30 kg., two pens were used. In addition to the normal, mainly home-grown feed consisting of cereal chaff, potatoes and green waste, one lot was given 10 g. of dried cow manure per animal per day. The other lot received 10 g. of cow manure treated with the preparation in dry condition. During the course of a fairly protracted fermentation period, microbial conditions arise under which certain vitamins and antibiotic substances are formed, and these can be of great importance, especially for pigs. For under natural conditions pigs seek out such substances in woods and fields. It is now known that large quantities of vitamins of the B group, for example, are formed in healthy humus[12].

In practical pig rearing, the useful results of feeding with humus components have long been generally known. Grass sods were given to young pigs, and cow manure has been found to be of importance in maintaining the health of sows. It has even been found useful to keep breeding sows and cattle together in the same field, for bovine stomachs and intestines produce vital substances that the pig can utilise (folic acid, biotin, cobalamine, vitamin K).

The present experiments involved a chromatographic procedure for the semi-quantitative determination of amino acids in the urine[13,14]. Chromatographic tests using benzidine on glucuronic acid were also made[15]. In addition, comparative chromatographic tests of the urine were made using silver lactate[13,14,16]. Feeding with the different supplements over a period of seven days gave continuous differences in the amino acid pattern and in the silver lactate chromatograms.

Table I	One-dimensional Amino Acid Test Mean of 7 days in mg/litre urine, semi-quantitative	
	Using 10 g combined prep.	Using 10 g manure
Cystine	5	5
Lysine	12	9
Histidine	36	30
Arginine	8	7
Aspartic acid	53	37
Glycine	78	54
Threonine	34	24
Glutamic acid	88	56
Alanine	34	26
Tyrosine	43	31
Valine	8	3
Methionine	6	4
Tryptophan	+	+
Phenylalanine	8	6
Leucine	3	1

Daily weight gains per animal:

Combined preparation	412 g.	
Cow manure only	372 g.	

With the herbal preparations (hereafter referred to as the combined preparation), an enhancement of the colour of the silver lactate ascending chromatograms was apparent, indicating that the animals can cope with the feedstuffs more easily and that their metabolism suffers no undue degree of nitrogen retention. Averaged over seven days, the chromatographic amino acid analyses showed higher values for aspartic acid, lysine, threonine, glutamic acid and tyrosine, in so far as this could be detected in a one-dimensional test.

27

However, a disturbance in the feeding occurred during this period. Owing to the partial fermentation of the green fodder they received, the animals got diarrhoea. The disturbance was less marked in those receiving the combined preparation than in the other group.

The experiment was then broken off and after a 10-day break was replaced by an intensive fattening regime using a precisely calculated feed consisting of soya meal, steamed fishmeal and barley meal supplemented with potatoes. In this second experimental period lasting five days the 18 animals ate:

| | | | Per pig per day | |
	18 pigs for 5 days	Total	Protein content	Starch content
Potatoes	225 kg	2.5 kg	35 g	600 g
Barley meal	45 kg	0.5 kg	43 g	350 g
Soya meal	18 kg	0.2 kg	80 kg	150 g
Fishmeal (steamed)	13.5 kg	0.15 kg	75 g	110 g
			233 g	1210 g

Fodder Ration

In this experiment the animals were divided into three groups:

- Group 1 received a daily supplement of 10 g. of the combined preparation per animal.
- Group 2 received only the feed without any supplement.
- Group 3 received a daily supplement of 10 g. of dried cow manure per animal.

Each animal consumed 2.8 litres of water a day.

Their mean weight was 35 kg.

The gain in weight of the pigs over the five days was 89.5 kg.

The results of the urine analyses were expressed even more consistently in this experimental period. The silver lactate chromatograms were clearer and brighter, and there was a clear subdivision of the upper horizons into fine transverse bands indicating liver and intestinal activity.

The chromatographic analyses of amino acids again revealed relatively high values in the aspartic acid, glycine, threonine, glutamic acid, alanine and tyrosine regions.

Table II	One-dimensional amino acid test Mean of 5 days in mg/litre urine, semi-quantitative		
	Combined prep.	Manure	No supplements
Cystine	27	17	16
Lysine	32	11	15
Histidine	72	52	60
Aspartic acid	58	45	42
Glycine	90	60	65
Threonine	31	15	18
Glutamic acid	120	78	52
Alanine	32	20	15
Tyrosine	21	13	15
Valine	11	7	6
Methionine	7	6	4
Tryptophan	+	+	+
Phenylalanine	9	8	8

There are clear indications throughout that internal respiration was better in the animals receiving the combined preparation, and that the endocrine activity of the pituitary gland, the thyroid and the adrenal glands proceeded with less disturbance. This may be of considerable importance in the control of electrolyte balance (sodium-calcium). The pH of the body fluids and serum of the pig needs to lie in the middle range, deviations in the direction of either acidosis or alkalosis being attended by serious dangers. Such conditions can usually be detected at an earlier stage in the pH of the urine[17,18].

The pH values of the animals receiving the combined preparation as a feed supplement lay between 6.2 and 6.5, while in the control animals they were rather higher, with greater deviations in both directions. The pH values of the animals receiving manure as a feed supplement lay between 5.8 and 6.3. On keeping the urine for observation for a number of days, it appeared that the urine of the animals receiving the combined preparation was very stable, showing little change and retaining a spicy, flowery odour. It is known that the odour of urine can be very informative. For example, a paediatrician can tell from the smell of a child's urine whether the child has received mother's milk and also whether it has been properly fed in other respects. The urines of the other animals soon became cloudy, decomposed very much more quickly and soon began to smell foul.

The amino acid chromatogram bands of the pigs receiving the combined preparation were harmonious and clean. The others had yellow specks in the aspartic acid, tyrosine and methionine regions, indicating nitrogen retention and incomplete breakdown of protein components. Under such conditions the feedstuffs are penetrating too far into the corporeal nature and into the body fluids. In the long term this leads to toxicity[19] and inhibition of the internal glands, which can be very detrimental to the quality of the meat.

The increase in live weight was very marked. All the animals showed a very high increase, as was to be expected with the intensive fattening diet adopted. The increase was exceptionally high in the animals receiving no supplement and in those receiving the manure, amounting to 1050 g. per animal daily at a live weight of 40 kg.

Decomposition of Urine at Room Temperature Increase in pH values, 2 animals per test		
	Combined preparation	Manure	No supplements
1st day	0.4 pH	0.9 pH	1.2 pH
2nd day	0.35	0.7	0.5
6th day	0.7	1.5	1.5

Increase in pH is an indicator of urine decomposition through putrefaction. The lowest increase in pH was recorded in the animals receiving the combined preparation.

The weight increase here indicates a risk of nitrogen retention.

The group receiving the combined preparation had a daily increase of 800 g. per animal at a live weight of 40 kg. This is an optimal increase for this body weight[20] and entails no risk of disturbance or internal disorders.

The experiments were concluded on 2nd November and the 18 animals returned to the normal farm feeding programme.

As a check on any after-effects of the feed supplements, urine samples were again collected and examined on 9th November, and the pigs were also weighed.

The free amino acid chromatograms of the urine from the animals that had received the combined preparation up to 2nd November still showed higher values in the lysine, histidine, aspartic acid and threonine regions. And when the urine of these animals was allowed to stand for several days, it again differed from that of the other two groups in decomposition, turbidity and smell. The group receiving no supplement and that receiving manure hardly differed from one another. The increase in weight was far greater in the animals that had received the combined preparation. A clear after-effect was therefore evident.

31

After-effects of Supplementary Feeding with 10 g. Combined Preparation Daily per Animal, in Three Pigs per test

	Combined prep.	Dried manure	No supplements
pH of urine	6.15	6.7	6.9
Increase in pH after 5 days' decomposition	0.35	1.1	1.1
Specific gravity	1.006	1.009	1.008
Daily weight gain per pig over 10 days	422 g	288 g	286 g

The animals receiving the combined preparation lay more peacefully and rootled around less in the manure, even long after the conclusion of the supplementary feeding.

The test demonstrated that daily application of 1 g. of prepared herbs per animal resulted in marked differences.

Processing enables the herbs to acquire very different qualities. It appears that protein components are formed during fermentation that are not observed during normal rotting processes. These increases in protein are an expression of life processes and as such they are very important and indeed crucial for both the quality and effectiveness of the preparation. They may arise in a variety of ways.

The analyses of herbal composts presented here, together with the urine analyses, reveal a wide new field for research on living inter-relationships between soil, plant and animal.

The results of the tests suggest that hormone production in the humus is improved through the addition of the prepared herbs, and that the hormones are also of importance to plants grown on manures containing them. In the soil these hormones may be destroyed very quickly, especially with heavy mechanical cultivation. It is necessary to learn the art of regulating the decomposition of organic fertilisers in such a way as to retain the greatest possible amounts of hormones[21].

The effect of the humus materials derived from herbs on the feeding of pigs may be likened to that of antibiotics. However, there is an important difference, in that in the present case none of the complications associated with antibiotic treatment arise.

The difference depends on the mode of preparation. On the one hand, there is a complete separation from the normal processes of nature since pure cultures are used. On the other hand, we have wide-ranging combinations and living relationships which in themselves make for harmony and hence are not disruptive.

The use of antibiotics is known to entail the following risks: dihydrostreptomycin can cause irreversible deafness; sizable doses of penicillin and streptomycin irritate the cortex of the brain; chlorotetracyclin given intravenously in doses above 2 g. or orally above 3 g. has a toxic effect on the liver; bacitracin, polymycin and neomycin cause serious damage to the kidneys; allergies are sometimes induced by antibiotics; and the equilibrium of the intestinal flora is often disturbed, leading to over-development of microorganisms that cause diarrhoea.

It is often observed that eczemas (mycoses) re-appear. Ninety percent of the fungi associated with these belong to the species *Candida albicans*.

The disturbances of the intestinal flora result in changes in intestinal vitamin synthesis and consequently also in the internal metabolism. Intestinal necroses arise and meat quality is altered. With broad-spectrum antibiotics in particular, such as tetracyclin, there is a marked alteration in the intestinal flora after three days: coliform bacteria and the like, *Clostridium* and white staphylococci decline, while *Proteus, Pseudomonas aeruginosa*, pathogenic streptococci and other staphylococci multiply. This sometimes leads to persistent diarrhoea.

Thus many unforeseen difficulties may arise. Especially to be feared is the development of pathogen resistance, leading to serious dangers under hospital conditions.

None of these risks are to be feared with the humus materials used in the work described here. Over against the use of antibiotic treatments in agriculture we can set a new way of regulating life processes, a way which is more in tune with nature. This can be expected to have very considerable effects, even on meat quality.

Chapter Four

Silica in Agriculture: An Essential in Successful Farming and also a Therapy

Around the turn of the century, Professor Partsch, geheimrat and director of the Geological Institute of Breslau, arranged for Dr. W. Remer to investigate the advances in fruit and wine production in the eastern regions of Germany. It turned out that, east of the River Elbe, the success of fruit and wine growing was closely associated with sandy soils. In the then state of knowledge of the relationships between soil, plant and climate, this represented a significant advance.

It was the disadvantages of sandy soils that were more familiar to farmers in the east. The broad sandy plains east of the Elbe were a perpetual problem child for the owners of big estates. Sandy soils formed extensive stretches of more or less marginal land in the endangered agricultural zone 7,* the largest and poorest of the former German agricultural zones. Even recent developments in agricultural chemistry had failed to be of use, and in 1921 the then minister of agriculture, Warmbold, put forward a plan for the reforestation of one million hectares of sandy arable land. The prevailing view was that nothing but the application of artificial fertilisers could make these sandy soils worth cultivating. On the soils of agricultural zone 7, which were not merely sandy but also dry, the reverse had indeed been demonstrated. But because the sandy soils had often failed under chemical farm management,

---

*In Germany, soils are classified by numbers, according to their types.

the value of these soils fell and interest in them declined more and more.

At the time of the settlement of the eastern region, the situation was such that the settlers occupied the loamy soils and left the sandy soils to the Slav farmers. Slav and Wend farmers in some areas knew very well how to manage sandy soils. The Wend smallholder of Lausitz and the Spreewald, who even today, undisturbed, retains his own culture side by side with the German culture, was a real master on sandy soils. His resources were cow dung as a basis for manuring, cattle as draught animals for working the flat land and continuous French ploughing or subsoiling (Rigolen) of the light, dry sandy soils. It sounds very simple, but it conceals not a little wisdom. Subsoiling means aeration of the soil to a depth of 50 to 70 cm. without displacing the soil layers. Prince Pückler used the art of subsoiling as his principal means of converting the Muskau and Branitz heathland into a park of 7000 Morgen (c. 1750 ha) within a short time[23].

So even sandy soils, if they are maintained in a living way, can produce very good results. Rarely, however, has it proved possible to make sandy soils really productive.

Destruction of Sandy Soils by Sun and Heat[24]

When sandy soils fail to yield a crop, this is not due to an absolute nutrient deficiency. A sand of the kind found around Berlin between Gesundbrunnen and Neucöln, contains the following:

> 80.86% quartz
> 15.70% feltdspar (with 14–15% potash)
> 1.95% calcium carbonate[25]

36

Feldspar, when it is in colloidal solution and helps form a crumb structure in the living soil, can be a bearer of fertility. It contains all the essential plant nutrients. But a sandy soil has a granular structure, and because an uncovered sandy soil heats up readily and absorbs light strongly, the development of its soil life is impeded.

According to Taderko[26] the heat conductivity of sand is thirty-five times as great as that of loam. Sand heats up quickly and quickly releases the absorbed heat again. Quartz sand and glass are traditionally used as building materials for country bread ovens. Clayey loam is used as the outer coating and holds the warmth while inside the oven the sand radiates the heat on to the bread.*

When a sandy soil is left to itself, its ready absorption of heat unfortunately has more disadvantages than advantages. Even under mild March sunshine the soil warms up quickly and at night it cools down equally fast. Such marked differences in heat are death to delicate root tissues. Temperature variations of 20 to 30°C between midday and midnight are not infrequent on sandy soils with a thin plant cover. During the summer months the temperature on a sandy soil with little plant cover can rise to above 50°C[27]. Soil organisms perish under such conditions, and their decomposition leads to the formation of acids, which attack the soil and cause leaching. It is quite

---

*According to Taderko, heat conductivity at 50°C is

0.000208 for loam
0.00717 for sand

Heat conductivity is equal to the amount of heat in calories that flows through 1 cm. in 1 sec. when the difference in temperature over the distance of 1 cm. is 1°. The heat conductivity of sand can be almost doubled by trampling and compressing. Heat conductivity is high in material with a high silica content; hence sand heats up and cools down quickly and shows large variations in temperature.

an experience to see how strongly a sandy soil heats up during a summer drought. Our own numerous measurements in the Mark* have shown that in the top 1–2 cm. of soil in open sandy sites the temperature rises to 60°C during the summer months. On immediately adjacent sandy soils with a plant cover, temperatures measured at the same time were only 20–25°C, occasionally 30°C. But the heat from the open sites spreads outwards to affect the surrounding areas. The reflected heat warms the air and drives it upwards, giving rise to vortices. These then help to complete the destruction of the soil surface membrane. The soil is robbed of its last drop of water. And with the loss of soil water, all fertility likewise disappears. Instead of earthworms and other useful soil organisms, ants, ant lions and spiders make their appearance and render even poorer the granular structure of the soil. In the course of the year an ever-increasing encroachment of sand and drifting of soil may be observed. The final phase is dune formation.

All this goes to confirm the opinion that sand is something of a superfluous gift in agriculture.

Silica, Transmitter of Heat and Light Activity

Not only heat but also light is transmitted by silica. Silica is permeable to both the quantities and the qualities of heat and light. Wood-burning ovens show this quite clearly. Quartz sand is thus able, according to the regional type of landscape, to transmit characteristic climatic and atmospheric heat and light conditions. It is extremely difficult to demonstrate the qualitative properties of silica in strictly defined scientific experiments.

In no way is it possible to use silica as an agricultural

---

*Mark is a region of Germany.

fertiliser like other substances. It cannot be used to produce any commercially profitable fertiliser.

Lili Kolisko was the first to take up Rudolf Steiner's anthroposophical statements on silica. By adding sand to pot plants in a darkened trench, she showed that the effect of light was enhanced by the silica.

A study of this work on silica readily reveals the difficulties of quantitative determination, and one can only admire the originality of Lili Kolisko's experimental design. At the same time, however, working with silica teaches one the inadequacy of plot trials constructed on a purely quantitative basis. The results of a single year in a field trial can never be a determining factor for the following year. In terms of the experimental science of today and yesterday, true exactness allows only retrospective and not predictive conclusions to be drawn from normal plot trials. Life however does not permit such one-sidedness, hence we are thus transferring to the future the conclusions that really only apply to the past.

Sandy Soils and Quality

In working with silica, new factors occur to the alert observer. There are obvious connections with organic decay. This is sufficiently clear from the rapid build-up and decline of sandy soils. In addition, silica influences the life cycle. This is expressed in the quality of the crops from fertile sandy soils. Oats from healthy sandy soils have the properties and grain quality of mountain oats. Rye from such soils is appreciated for its thin husk and good baking quality, and fruit becomes particularly aromatic. But all these valued characteristics only appear on living sandy soils, in other words, they are associated with the total life cycle.

The work with silica has revealed two important factors

in agriculture which have been totally neglected by the agricultural chemists in their fertiliser experiments with salts: one is the effect of silica on organic decomposition and the other its effect on the life cycle.

Heath Sand and Podsol Formation
Influence of Sand on Organic Decomposition

In order to understand the influence of silica on organic decomposition, let us first look at its negative effect. On all *wet* sandy soils that are not cultivated with special care, a highly acid form of decomposition of organic matter develops through the action of soil fungi. The soil becomes filled with dark peaty products of decomposition, which must not be confused with humus. This is how the highly nitrogen-deficient black sandy soils arise, the wet podsols. They are extremely infertile and present enormous problems of farm management. They cry out for nitrogen fertilisers. But if they are treated with nitrogenous salts, other fertiliser requirements and deficiency symptoms soon manifest themselves. This has been demonstrated by Russian agricultural chemists, for whom the study of such soils, which cover wide tracts of northern and central Russia, has been of great importance. Even classical soil scientists formed the opinion that these soils could only be tackled with farmyard manure[29]. But farmyard manure is consumed very rapidly by these soils and has no lasting effect, in contrast to its effect on loam and loess soils. The only remedy is to compost the farmyard manure and to build up humus material by composting plant remains together with bonemeal, hair and wool waste, lime, peat, dung and liquid manure. It is important to break down the infertile, nitrogen-poor carbon compounds of the black sandy soils by means of living, protein-rich fertilisers and legume culture, and to build up a true humus through the inclusion of perennial grasses in the rotation. This applies also to the sandy heathland soils of the western Elbe region.

In this sandy west Elbe heathland, it is a question of altering the water level of the soil. Because a podsol with impervious horizons has developed, the soil is subject to standing water in winter and to disturbed capillarity and desiccation in summer.

Now when some loam is present in the soil, conditions change immediately. Water movement in the soil is quite different, as is soil aeration. Constant soil moisture and constant aeration are the prerequisites for neutral decomposition. That is a lesson that has gradually been learnt in the course of compost-making. Correct soil moisture is as important in humus formation as in plant growth. In Winter, when the sandy soil becomes waterlogged above the compacted layer, no humus but only an acid wet peat is formed. In Summer, on the other hand, the soil tends to form an acid dry peat. Under such conditions, sand is in no way able to develop its qualitative properties.

Besides such measures as composting and improvement by planting, sandy soils can also be improved when waste from clay-beds and quarries, and grindings from artificial stone factories (especially from feldspar-containing rock) and marl are mixed in during compost making. An admixture of clay and feldspar to quartz sand is the old recipe for porcelain with a fine resonance. In the porcelain industry, too, knowledge and experience have been more important than scientific mastery.

Silica in the Self-contained Farm Organism

In order to evaluate properly the role of silica in the natural cycle, it is necessary to know something of the early evolution of the earth's organism. In earlier periods,

41

silica had a very different significance for the living world from what it has now. It had the role of preparing the way for the physical materialisation of the various kingdoms of nature. The primitive siliceous rocks, such as quartzite, schists and greywacke, are carbon-bearing rocks, i.e. they once existed in an abundantly life-filled state.

It is only through what has been said by spiritual science regarding the earth's evolution that it has been possible to perceive the extreme importance of silica.

On this basis it is possible to work with the idea of a self-contained farm organism even on the poorest of sandy soils. Previously, hardly anyone would have dared to establish a self-sufficient farm on such so-called nutrient-deficient sandy soils, making use as far as possible only of farm-produced manures and of the existing soil conformation, as has been done at Marienhöhe near Bad Saarow/ Mark. The acidity and calcium deficiency of the soil alone would appear to make it impossible to avoid treating it with lime[30].

Nevertheless, remarkable results were observed in the development of bone and hide in the cattle herd. The animals acquired glossy coats, healthy skin, a lively expression, good horn growth and also strong bone development. Indeed, the further development of the herd even showed an increase in fertility and the evolution of a distinct individual character with excellent heritability.

Silica and the Feeding Cycle

As soon as successful neutralisation of acid sandy soils has been achieved through composting, the straw harvested from it for fodder acquires the value of *hay*. This was known to older farmers[31] and has been observed time and again during the conversion of light soils.

Fodder plants on poor soils are not characterised by a

high calcium content. Nevertheless, animals raised within a healthy, self-contained farm cycle under just such conditions develop thick hides and strong bone. The so-called robust type develops which, besides its robustness, maintains a consistent performance and retains its toughness and physical liveliness up to a late age.

Understandably, the farmer has an interest in the mineral composition of the fodder he gives his animals. Here a remarkable fact may be noted. The calcium-rich skeletal framework of our domestic animals is far more fully developed than that of the human being. From this it might be supposed that our domestic animals should receive nutriment with an especially high content of bases and calcium. Closer investigation makes it clear, however, that most of the fodders provided, such as hay, straw and green fodder, contain *no mineral* in such quantities *as silica*. The hay from non-acid, neutral areas contains appreciably more silica than that from acid areas.

According to Schneidewind:

Good meadow hay contains 27.2 g. silicic acid per 1000 g.
Acid meadow hay contains 13.8 g. silicic acid per 1000 g.

When a neutral humus decomposition has been achieved on grassland and arable land through composting and soil tillage, what must be taken into account is that the ash content of the component plants increases, that species with a high ash content multiply and that the yield of silica likewise increases. The silica-rich grasses must of course be complemented by base-rich legumes. Fodder legumes and their straw have an ash content comprising two-thirds basic substances and about 10% of silicic acid. The proportions are reversed in fodder grasses and their straw.

43

Content in the ash:

I. Roughage	Percentage silicic acid
Good hay	37
Drained peatland hay	7
Reclaimed coastal marsh hay	44
Rye straw	64
Wheat straw	63
Spelt straw	70
Oat straw	52
Barley straw	50
II. Root crops	
Potatoes	3.6
Carrots	8.7
Fodder Beet	3.5

The contents of potassium and phosphates in plants can be increased by fertilising with potassium and phosphate. But *no* increase in silica content can be expected from scattering silica powder, or crushed quartz. Silica cannot be used to make an artificial fertiliser in the normal sense of the word. Only a few cases are known in which heated, finely ground silicates applied to active soils have had a direct effect on growth. Such effects can be startling and powerful. But in general silica has no direct fertilising effect. It is for this reason that its role in the balance of nature has been neglected and forgotten. We have to consult earlier writings if we are to find information on this problem.

In their *Ökonomische Chemie (Economic Chemistry)* of 1842, Professors Duflos and Hirsch[32] report that the silica present in plants is in a form which is partly soluble and partly insoluble. The ratio of soluble to insoluble differs in different plants.

Species	Soluble silicic acid %	Insoluble silicic acid %
St Lucie's cherry	1.0	1.8
Red elder	0.2	3.2
Hazel branches	0.5	4.2
Mulberry branches	1.0	13.1
Laburnum	1.78	8.0
Norway spruce from France, wood	1.0	8.0
Norway spruce from Norway, wood	2.0	13.0
Fur, wood	1.73	4.6
Rye straw	35.0	75.0

The table shows that silica content and solubility are dependent on both species and site. It may be assumed that not only content of silica but also its solubility has a lasting effect on our domestic animals. It is surely detrimental to feed breeding pigs on fodders that are decidedly low in silica, such as fishmeal and root crops. Far more emphasis should be laid on supplementary feeding with hay seed and chaff. Chaff has a 70–80% silica content in the ash.

Silica balance, which is emerging as an ever more important health factor, has been drastically disturbed by modern agriculture. The use of artificial fertilisers leads to a decline in the silica content of crop plants[33].

In 1939 the Würzburg physiologist Linzel showed how the mineral content of agricultural feeds had changed during the preceding 100 years through the intervention of modern agriculture[34]. A comparison of the figures for 1896 and 1932 shows that a marked increase, up to threefold, in the potassium content of roughage and root crops and a decrease in magnesium content have taken place. Silica was not included in these studies. For this we must turn to even earlier work, and compare the findings of Duflos

& Hirsch (1842) with those of Schneidewind in 1930. Here, too, a sharp rise in potassium leaps to the eye. Total ash contents have changed and the *silica content* of the ash has fallen by *up to 30%*.

		Per 100 parts dry matter					Silica per 100 parts
Plant species	**Ash**	**K_2O+Na_2O**	**CaO**	**MgO**	**P_2O_5**	**SiO_2**	**plant ash**
Wheat straw							
old (1842)	3.52	0.05	0.24	0.03	0.17	2.87	80.0
new (1930)	4.96	0.96	0.28	0.11	0.20	3.10	62.0
Rye straw							
old	2.80	0.04	0.18	0.01	0.17	2.29	81.0
new	3.90	1.10	0.29	0.09	0.26	1.88	48.0
Barley straw							
old	5.24	0.23	0.55	0.08	0.16	3.86	74.0
new	4.49	1.50	0.33	0.09	0.20	2.34	52.0
Oat straw							
old	5.74	0.87	0.15	0.02	0.01	4.58	79.0
new	6.45	2.00	0.38	0.12	0.35	3.00	47.0
Pea haulm							
old	5.00	0.23	2.73	0.34	0.24	0.39	19.0
new	3.91	0.68	1.82	0.27	0.35	0.29	7.4
Bean haulm							
old	3.22	0.70	0.62	0.02	0.22	0.22	7.0
new	4.47	2.02	1.20	0.26	0.29	0.32	7.2

Changes in Mineral Content over 88 Years

Everything that has by degrees been ascertained about silica should make this marked decline in silica content a matter of some concern. But mere quantitative considerations are in no way adequate for an understanding of the significance of silica. For the value of silica lies precisely in the fact that while on the one hand it occurs in material form in a certain equilibrium, i.e. it changes very little but at the same time transmits valuable natural forces to the living world, on the other hand it influences organic processes more strongly when it is in high dilutions (see p. 00). A comprehensive and effective mobilisation of silica should therefore under no circumstances be omitted from the farm cycle. To what extent this is the norm is apparent from the following table, which presents the ash and silica content of various sorts of roughage (after Mentzel & Lengerke).

Plant species	% ash in dry matter	% SiO in dry matter	% SiO in ash
1. Hay			
Meadow hay	74.8	27.2	36.0
Hay from reclaimed coastal marsh	75.9	33.8	44.0
Hay from drained deep sphagnum soils	58.4	3.5	6.0
Hay from sour wet meadows	36.8	13.8	37.5
Hay from sewage irrigation	74.6	6.8	9.4
2. Legumes			
Lucerne (alfalfa)	62.9	5.9	9.4
Red clover	46.2	3.0	6.5
Serradella	86.1	7.0	8.6
3. Straw			
Winter rye straw	39.3	18.8	47.7
Winter wheat straw	48.6	31.0	64.0
Spring rye straw	42.0	25.0	60.0
Barley straw	44.9	23.4	52.0
Oats straw	64.5	30.0	46.5
4. Legume haulm			
Field bean haulm	44.7	3.2	7.2
Pea haulm	39.1	2.9	7.4

It should be taken into account that the full silica content in the plant is only achieved in the final weeks of development. The first cut of hay is higher in silica than the second. According to Schneidewind, the aftermath contains only about half as much silica as the first cut. All fodders having the nature of shade plants, such as grass grown under irrigation with sewage (see table above), are low in silica. Even if high in mass, the fodder value of 'shade' forage plants and of forced forage plants is lower than that of 'light' and 'sun' forages. Detailed information on this is available from mountain farms on sites with different slopes and aspects.

It is very important to promote the uptake of silica. It is not enough for the plant merely to be fully exposed to the light; the soil itself must also be healthy. The production of organic silica within the natural economy is an extraordinary achievement both for the plant and for the soil. Liebig himself worked on silica uptake[35]. He attributed soil exhaustion largely to the inability of the soil to make enough silica available to the plant. His experiments included the following. He determined the silica content of samples taken from an oat field on 3rd July and then repeated the test on 18th August shortly before maturity. Up to 3rd July, silica uptake was 18.8 kg per quarter hectare. At this date the oats had 29% silica in the ash. By 27th August the silica uptake was 72.5 kg per quarter hectare and the silica content of the plant ash was 61%.

In the final growth period, the final six weeks, *silica uptake was 72.5 kg but nitrogen uptake only 7 kg* per quarter hectare. "Soil exhaustion can in no way be attributed to nitrogen," states Liebig. He points out, moreover, that a soil retains its fertility if the cereals grown on it are harvested while they are in flower, i.e. when silica uptake has not yet taken place but nitrogen uptake is largely complete. By 3rd July his oats had taken up 15.5 kg of nitrogen per quarter hectare. But the soil becomes exhausted only when the ripe grain is harvested. This does not happen when it has lost merely an additional 7 kg of nitrogen besides the 15.5 kg previously lost. What does it matter if an additional 7 kg are lost out of the 750 to 1250 kg of nitrogen that a soil of medium fertility contains? Normally a soil contains the same amount of phosphate and ten times as much potassium. The case is far otherwise for silica. It does indeed make up 48% of the earth's crust. But it is totally insoluble except when it is mobilised in the living organic cycle.

A real circulation of silica must be brought about by all the means available on the self-contained farm. It will then be possible for silica to develop its dynamic capacities.

Silica and Carbon, Pillars of the Agricultural Cycle

When considering essential nutrients in crop husbandry, we should deal first with carbon and then with silica. The dry matter of cereal plants consists of 30–40% carbon and 4% silicic acid, or 94% carbon compounds and 4% silicic acid. All the other elements make up only the remaining 2%. Making use of silica involves the whole soil-plant-animal cycle. Silica cannot be applied externally as a fertiliser. It always has to pass through the separate kingdoms of nature. To keep the silica moving, the living carbon cycle is necessary. This becomes clear even in composting organic waste. If we use a suitable kind of soil, we get the valuable humus silicates, the quartz compounds. But not every soil is suitable for mixing with farm-yard manure. Too great a ballast of mineral soil is to be avoided in composting. It is through the addition of living soil during composting that the valuable clay humus silicates arise on the one hand, and on the other the soluble humus substances which in high dilution stimulate root life[36]. The entry into solution of silicates is promoted by the soil microfauna. Earthworms, soil mites and crumb bacteria prepare the true soil, the humus, their activity being directed by the action of higher organisms. Carbon and silica are the two pillars of this occurrence. Forces of extraordinary value enter into the natural process by means of silica. By means of carbon they acquire form, and then, during growth, the whole process is raised from stage to stage. Silica attains a new level of life in the flowering plant, and in doing so develops a powerful activity which is connected with the plant's reproduction, with fruit formation and fertility. In cereals, it is through the assistance of the siliceous awns that flour and aroma are formed. In other plants silica enhances sugar and essential oils. The more subtle the processes become, the more the hexagon-forming *forces* of silica predominate over silica as *substance*. These are the forces that appear in the hexagonal quartz crystal and the hexagonal cell of the honeycomb. They are also expressed in the hexagonal crystals of honey. It is the forces of the flowering process, based on silica forces, that are active in restoring the metabolism of our domestic animals. The parts of the plant that still contain material silica sustain the formation of the skin and senses system. There is a wide span stretching from the hard siliceous rocks to the most delicate processes of honey formation and nectar yeasts which are of such value in maintaining the fertility of cattle. The hexagon-forming force is also present in milk when it curdles. It is even easier to detect in melted butter of good quality: when the melted butter cools, it crystallises in hexagonal form.

In feeding cattle, the point is not only to use silica in plant form but also to use the silica processes by feeding with dried herbs. In making a herbal brew*, use is made

*See footnote p. 107.

50

of the silica-containing awns and chaff of cereals as well as aromatic herbs. Favourable effects on skin development and butter fat formation have been demonstrated repeatedly from this.

Unquestionably, we must distinguish between the application of silica in rather crude form, and the processes involving silica in homoeopathic form, for the latter are those that sustain a healthy capacity for reproduction and fertility and thus enable the farm organism to achieve good productivity. In the processes in which silica is in the homoeopathic state, it acts as an organising element within the self-contained farm organism. Via a cosmic-earthly fertilisation process, it is by means of silica that the farm property can unite to form a single individuality with a character of its own.

The above indications of the role of silica in various spheres of development allow us to put it to use in the changing, growing and self-renewing life cycle of the self-contained farm, and a totally new therapy for agriculture is the result. Silica becomes a decisive component in the success of a farm and at the same time a source of healing for soil, plant, animal and man.

Chapter Five

Application of Homoeopathic Silica to Plants

In 1924 Rudolf Steiner gave agriculture not only some utterly new insights into the importance of silica in the metabolism of soil, plant and animal, but also practical suggestions as to its use, in particular the application of homoeopathic rock crystal to green plants. Silica, though making up 48% of the earth's crust, had at that time received little attention as a factor in the balance of nature.

As a brief introduction to the problem, a series of publications on the matter may be mentioned[37].

Experiments conducted from 1928 to 1952 by Dr. E. Bartsch on the sandy soils of Marienhöhe, near Bad Saarow, Mark/Brandenburg, have given a constant practical stimulus and have resulted in deeper involvement in problems relating to silica[37].

Over a period of 40 years, on farms and gardens that have followed the ideas presented at Koberwitz, use had been made of finely ground rock crystal which had been subjected to an enlivening warmth process and applied in a homoeopathic state. Much remains to be done, however, as regards more extensive, research-oriented work.

For this reason, new investigations were undertaken in 1963, in Stuttgart.

Preliminary trials with the silica preparation (501)* were conducted in the first year. These involved taking 4–5 g.

---

*The investigations were carried out with the assistance of Dr. G. Remer. This preparation is often called "horn-silica."

finely ground rock crystal that had been kept throughout the summer in a cow horn buried in the ground. This was stirred for one hour and sprayed onto 1000 m² plots of oats and rye. The rock crystal had been ground for different lengths of time, in some cases by hand, in others in a laboratory grinder. Particle sizes of 7 micron and less were obtained. No differences associated with method of grinding were detected.

The following year (1964) the possible role of different types of silica on the effectiveness of treatment was examined in single applications. The quartz materials used in the preparation of the silica (501) and applied on various experimental farms were as follows:

1. Silicic acid glass, made from Brazilian quartz.
2. Silicic acid glass, made from tetrachlorite ($SiCl_4$).
3. Actinolite $Ca_2Mg_5Si_8O_{22}(OH)_2$ from Silvretta-Stausee, Austria.
4. Serpentine $Mg_6Si_4O_{10}(OH)_8$ from Val Malenko, Italian Alps.
5. Chalcedony.
6. Diatomaceous earth (Kieselguhr), partly transformed to cristobalite through heat treatment.
7. Rose-quartz from Arendal, Norway.

When used on cereals, samples 2 and 7 appeared visually somewhat superior.

These tests, however, did not really give measurable values: weight determinations of treated cereal strips in the field proved too laborious.

Consequently, the 1965 treatments were mainly continued on horticultural land protected from the wind, the crops under investigation (wheat, rye and brassicas) being treated up to 12 times with the silica preparation (501). Extracts from the green plants were analysed chromatographically on filter paper in conjunction with metallic salts, using the differential method developed principally by Lili Kolisko but worked out initially in 1903 by the Russian Tswett as a method of absorption analysis[38].

Here there were clear disparities between the extracts of treated and untreated plants, indicating differences in content of dicarboxylic acids. These acids participate in the internal respiratory cycle, contributing to the formation of carbohydrates, fats and proteins.

Similarly, chromatographic analysis of free amino acids revealed differences in aspartic acid, glutamic acid* and alanine. The three years' work thus resulted in a possible test method, and it was decided to repeat the successful garden plot tests in the field in 1966.

Experiments in 1965

Free amino acids were determined semi-quantitatively in a one-dimensional descending chromatography test with a mixture of methylethylketone and propionic acid, ninhydrin being used for colour development. These tests are merely indicative; but when used as a series they provide not only clear illustrative material but also controls.

Amino acids in extract of Savoy cabbage, in mg./litre				
	With silica D7		Untreated	
Date	Sept 6	Sept 8	Sept 6	Sept 8
Aspartic acid	120	120	80	80
Glutamic acid	180	200	110	150
Alanine	40	50	15	25

Other organic acids are also continually being formed in plants. The process is intimately connected with the internal respiratory metabolism which, like the Krebs cycle

---

*Aspartic acid and glutamic acid are monoamino-dicarboxylic acids.

in human and animal organisms, forms an essential basis for anabolic and catabolic processes in plants[39]. In apples, for example, the content of organic acids declines and sugar concentration rises during the course of ripening.

The dicarboxylic acids commonly present in plants give rise to columnar forms on analysis by differential chromatography with metallic salts. Extracts from Savoy cabbage treated six times with silica preparation 501 had more of such columns than extracts from untreated plants—an expression of internal respiratory processes.

Experiments in 1966

In 1966, with a view to opening up the practical application of homoeopathic silica and facilitating its use where stirring for an hour is not feasible, experiments mainly with the seventh potency were carried out on vegetable fields. In each case, rock crystal that had been prepared in a cow horn (i.e. 501) was ground together with lactose for an hour 4 times to produce the fourth potency. The fourth potency was converted to the seventh potency by shaking with water, each time for $2^1/2$ minutes. The quantity sprayed per quarter hectare was 30 litres. This procedure readily enables *200 litres*, at a dilution of D7, to be produced from 200 g. of the D4 silica in three further stages of potentising *in only 20 minutes*.

Unless otherwise indicated, the preparation used in these experiments of 1966 was 501 homoeopathically potentised to Si D7. The experimental plots were treated once a week when the weather was fine, usually in the afternoon. The work in Spring was initially started off in the garden again, in order to see whether the results of 1965 could be repeated.

Treatment of Savoy cabbage and of caraway in its second year gave rise to clear differences in development. The treated caraway had shorter stems and fuller umbel formation. The Savoy cabbage was firmer and ready for harvesting earlier. Extracts from the Savoy cabbage again showed clear differences in aspartic acid, glutamic acid and alanine. Chromatographic differentiation of the extracts with silver lactate and sodium hydroxide revealed stronger columnar formations in the treated plants, indicating an increase in dicarboxylic acids.

Next came the question of whether the results on a larger scale in the field would be the same as in the garden. Trials with vegetable crops—kohlrabi, red cabbage and spring cabbage in May and June, and celeriac, leeks, carrots and turnips later in the season—were set up by the writer together with the horticultural inspector Miss Glashoff at Sottdorf, Klein-Süstedt and at Mönkloh. The main trials involved carrots, and most of the analyses were made on this crop.

In addition, garden trials were carried out on runner (pole) beans, dwarf beans, lettuce, smooth and curly endive, sugar loaf and curly kale, in each case on 10 m² plots.

Extracts were taken from the samples by means of an electric extractor (make: 'Progress') and tested as follows:

1. Aroma, taste, acid content (pH), potassium nitrate content.
2. Sugar content (in the carrots).
3. Iron content.
4. Free amino acids, analysed by descending chromatography.
5. Ascending chromatography with metallic salts.
6. Aging of extracts, as shown in ascending chromatograms with metallic salts for differentiation.

Taste and aroma can of course hardly be determined objectively, but clear differences appeared regularly and should therefore be mentioned. The extracts from plants treated several times were always clearly distinct from those from untreated plants. Taste and aroma in treated plant extracts were stronger and fuller, and lasted longer when the extract was allowed to stand.

Methods

Sugar content in the carrot extracts was determined semi-quantitatively using 'Merck Clinitest' tablets. For this procedure the carrot extracts were diluted. Potassium nitrate content was determined semi-quantitatively with diphenylamine according to the Morgan method[40]. The Morgan procedure was also used in soil analyses.

For the determination of iron content, use was made of the "Mercko test reagent." The method employs bathophananthroline-sulphonic acid.

In the free amino acid determinations, 0.04 ml. drops of extract were placed on strips of Whatman No. I filter paper and subjected to a descending chromatography procedure in special glass vessels; differentiation by methylethylketone and propionic acid was followed by spraying with ninhydrin and heat-drying[41]. Through comparison with standard solutions, semi-quantitative values could be read off according to the development of the colour spots.

Chromatography of extracts by means of Tswett's ascending procedure for analysis with metallic salts also gave pronounced characteristics. This method is readily modified. The carrot extract was diluted 1:5 and quantities of 1 ml. were allowed to rise on 16 cm. wide Whatman No. I papers. This was followed by 1 ml. of a 50% solution of Merck's lead acetate solution (1 + 9.DAB 15) and the paper was then dried in the dark. Subsequently 2 ml. silver lactate (0.25%) was allowed to rise through the paper. On exposure to light, the papers show a range of very varied forms. Dicarboxylic acids are clearly expressed in vertical, sometimes fanlike, columns and are an indication of the internal respiratory metabolism. As the extract ages, these characteristics fade away, indicating decomposition.

Trial Grounds and Trials

The soils available for the trials in Sottorf, Klein-Süstedt and Mönkloh were loamy sands with soil numbers of 25 to 35.* The turnip trial was carried out at Sottorf on a field with the following soil analysis on 10th July 1966:

					potassium	
			P_2O_5	K_2O	nitrate	lime
			mg per	mg per		
Depth	pH	N%	100 g	100 g	p.p.m.	t/ha
to 10 cm.	6.0	0.12	10	15	7	20
to 25 cm.	5.6	0.08	7	17	7	20
to 35 cm.	6.0	0.04	5	9	7	-

Betzendorfer Weg Field

The turnips were treated in two 100-metre strips, Si D7 being applied once a week over the period 15th August to 1st September 1966. The decomposition test and the iron test revealed clear differences. When left to stand, the extracts from untreated plants showed a greater increase in potassium nitrate:

---

*See footnote p. 35.

Aging Test, Potassium Nitrate in p.p.m.				
Turnips	Treated with Si D7		Untreated	
	Day 1	Day 3	Day 1	Day 3
Aug. 22 Sottorf	2	4	2	16
Sept. 1 Sottorf	2	2	2	16
Sept. 1 mineral fertiliser applied	-	-	4	12

Nitrates in vegetables can be converted to nitrites, and these when consumed block the respiratory enzymes and can cause methaemoglobinaemia in infants after 2–3 hours[42].

Carrot Tests

The main trials were carried out with carrots on 1000 m^2 plots in two fields at Klein-Süstedt. The two fields were cultivated in April and May and had both received the same organic manuring.

In external appearance there was hardly any difference between the treated and untreated plots. However, there were consistent differences in the successive analyses of the extracts. These showed the same trends for sugars, amino acids and chromatographic differentiation with metallic salts (indicating dicarboxylic acids).

Soluble sugar content in carrots is calculated as 4.3% sugar in diabetic diets.[46]

The higher sugar content of the treated carrots could always be tasted. When left to stand, the extract usually remained free from mould one day longer. This came to expression also in the chromatographic differentiation with metallic salts.

The results from these semi-quantitative determinations of free amino acids are in accordance with the opinion of

			P_2O_5 mg per 100 g	K_2O mg per 100 g	potas- sium nitrate p.p.m.	lime t/ha
Soil Analysis 15th July 1966						
Depth	**pH**	**N%**				
Field I. Loamy sand, soil number 20 to 25						
to 10 cm.	5.2	0.16	10	10	10	150
to 25 cm.	6.0	0.08	7	10	8	100
to 35 cm.	6.0	0.04	4.5	8	7	-
Field II. Loamy sand, soil number 25 to 35						
to 10 cm.	5.2	0.14	9.5	13	7	20
to 25 cm.	6.0	0.08	7.5	15	7	20
to 35 cm.	6.0	0.06	5.0	11	8	-

Field II was treated with Si D7 once a week from 23rd July to 28th August.

Composition of Carrots

Content according to Rein-Schneider (43)		Dicarboxylic acids according to Geigy (44)	
Water	88 g per 100 g	Malic acid	24mg%
Ash	0.7 g per 100 g	Citric acid	90mg%
Carbohydrates	9 g per 100 g	Oxalic acid	33 mg%
Crude fibre	1 g per 100 g		
Protein	1 g per 100 g		

Also present: caffeic acid, chlorogenic acid, ascorbic acid and 90 mg/g vitamin A. (45)

Professor Warburg, who says that amino acids such as aspartic acid, glutamic acid and alanine play a leading role in binding and reducing carbon dioxide following photo-synthesis[47].

According to Terentiev[48], it is now possible to synthe-sise asymmetric organic compounds with the aid of opti-cally active quartz. Some such process apparently takes

Sugar Analysis of Carrots (20–30 carrots per test) using Merck Clini-Test Tablets

Date	Repeated Si D7 treatment	Untreated
Carrots from Field I		
Aug. 8	3.2%	1.8%
Aug. 10	2.8%	1.6%
Aug. 17	3.8%	2.6%
Aug. 22	4.6%	4.0%
Aug. 26	4.4%	4.0%
Sept. 8	4.4%	3.8%
Oct. 6	4.6%	3.8%
Carrots from Field II		
Aug. 22	4.0%	3.6%
Aug. 26	3.8%	3.2%
Sept. 8	4.4%	4.0%
Carrots from Sottorf Garden		
Aug. 26	4.8%	4.0%
Carrots from Mönkloh treated 5 times with Si D7		
Sept. 2	3.6%	3.0%
treated 5 times with Si D6		
Sept. 2	3.8%	

Differences in flavour were also confirmed.

place when homoeopathic silica is applied to the green plant. The plant makes use of the most diverse plant acids in its internal metabolism and synthesising processes. These include not only the amino acids but also lactic acid, malic acid, citric acid, oxalic acid, fumaric acid, succinic acid, ketoglutaric acid, aconitic acid and other dicarboxylic acids.

A great variety of dibasic and tribasic organic acids become visible in the vertical differentiation of ascending chromatograms. Since these acids are only present in minute quantities in the total material, the tests require very

Amino Acid Analysis of Carrots, Semi-Quantitative, mg/litre					
	Repeated treatment with Si D7			Untreated	
	Aspartic acid	Glutamic acid	Alanine	Aspartic acid	Glutamic acid	Alanine
Carrots from Field I						
July 18	150	60	40	110	60	30
July 7	140	75	45	115	60	35
July 26	150	60	40	110	60	30
Aug. 3	140	60	35	110	40	25
Aug. 10	130	65	35	110	60	30
Aug. 17	135	70	35	110	40	30
Aug. 22	135	65	30	130	30	30
Aug. 26	135	65	35	120	40	20
Sept. 1	130	65	30	120	50	20
Sept. 8	135	65	35	120	50	20
Oct. 6	130	60	25	130	40	15
Carrots from Field II						
Aug. 22	130	75	30	130	55	30
Aug. 26	135	65	25	110	30	10
Sept. 1	135	70	30	130	40	25
Sept. 8	140	60	30	130	40	20

carefully graduated dilution and alkalinity control with sodium hydroxide. In extracts of carrot and all brassica crops it has however been possible to show an enhancement of acid metabolism following treatment with Si D7. Acid metabolism is controlled by a wide range of enzymes, and it appears that homoeopathic silica promotes the formation of the enzymes responsible for acid metabolism. On 29th November 1965, after the onset of frost, treated red cabbage showed no frost damage, in contrast to untreated.

Green vegetables and leaf vegetables were further tested for iron, using the method currently employed for serum iron determination in medicine. For this purpose, all glass vessels are kept overnight in a 50% solution of pure nitric acid and then rinsed twice in distilled water;

the filters also have to be cleaned with 10% hydrochloric acid and then rinsed twice with distilled water.

Four mg. trichloroacetic acid is used to remove the protein from 5 ml. of extract. 1 ml. is filtered off and treated with 1 ml. bathophenanthroline solution and examined photometrically[49].

Plants treated several times with Si D7 showed a somewhat higher iron content.

Iron determination has long been used in cereals as an indicator of quality.[50]

Here, too, the positive result of the iron test may be taken as an indication of a qualitative enhancement of protein processes. Protein synthesis in plants is usually associated with increased iron content.

Iron Content per kg. Dry Matter[51]	
High-iron plants	
Good hay	910 mg. Fe
Flowering perennial ryegrass	910 mg. Fe
Flowering yellow oatgrass	291–410 mg. Fe
Pea-vetch mixture	900–1400 mg. Fe
Soya beans	3080 mg. Fe
Low-iron plants	
Hay from sour land	46–300 mg. Fe
Yorkshire fog	25–160 mg. Fe
Meadow foxtail	66–85 mg. Fe
Marrowstem kale	118 mg. Fe
Green maize	216 mg. Fe

Bathophenanthroline Iron Test of Extracts (mg.%)		
	Repeated treatment with Si D7	Untreated
24.8 Turnips, Sottorf	140	110
Aug. 26 Turnips, Sottorf	140	110
Aug. 26 Turnips, mineral fertiliser, Bez.		80
Aug. 26 Turnips, mineral fertiliser, Diersbg.		90
Aug. 24 Curly kale, Sottorf garden	110	100
Aug. 24 Curly kale, mineral fertiliser		100
Aug. 24 Carrots, Kl. Sü. Field I	70	60
Aug. 24 Carrots, Kl. Sü. Field II	80	60
Sept. 1 Carrots, garden	80	80
Sept. 1 Curly kale, garden	110	110
Sept. 1 Endives, garden	120	110
Sept. 1 Sugar load, garden	125	115
Sept. 1 Turnips, Sottorf	130	120
Sept. 1 Turnips, Diersb.		90
Sept. 6 Celeriac, Mönkloh	120	105

Chemical analyses by means of chromatography with metallic salts provide further information. Extracts from plants treated repeatedly with Si D7 are again clearly distinguishable by the vertical columnar formations, which also appear with pure, highly diluted dicarboxylic acids. Citric acid, oxalic acid, malic acid and succinic acid, for example, always give formations of this kind on analysis with sodium hydroxide and silver lactate.

The investigations showed that a triple treatment with Si D7 or with preparation 501 stirred for one hour leads to clear changes in the plant extracts.

Application of the silica preparation also results in quantitative increases in yield. This was particularly apparent with runner beans, though not with dwarf beans. While the untreated runner beans had died off by 10th October, the treated plants still had uniformly green foliage at that date. This bears out completely the experience of Leihenseder[52]. In general, no yield determinations as such were undertaken, since quality aspects were the more important and the plots were in any case being picked for the regular supply of vegetables. But on 10th September 1966, in two 4 m² lots of carrots lifted from Field I as a sample, there was an 11% higher yield in the treated carrots. Thus with adequate organic management of the soil, it appears possible to influence yields of lettuce, cabbage and carrots even under garden conditions.

The investigations leave open a number of questions, namely those concerning pretreatment of the silica preparation, time of application, its effect on different plants and its effect under specific (mineral or organic) fertiliser treatments.

Summary

In accordance with suggestions made by Rudolf Steiner at Koberwitz in 1924, the effects of homoeopathic applications of specially prepared rock crystal on green plants were investigated, using extracts from treated and untreated plants.

The plants under investigation were: Savoy cabbage, caraway, runner beans, lettuce, sugar loaf, endive and curly kale under garden conditions and kohlrabi, other brassica crops, turnips, leeks, celeriac and carrots in the field.

With repeated treatments with the seventh potency of the silica preparation, i.e. at a dilution of 1 : 10 million, consistent changes in the plant extracts were demonstrated, despite the fact that silica is barely soluble in water. The treated plants not only had a stronger flavour and aroma but differed in free amino acids and in their behaviour with metallic salts when subjected to chromatographic tests. The more marked column formation in the chromatograms can be taken as an indication of more lively internal respiratory processes and dicarboxylic acid formation. Treated carrots contained more sugar, and green vegetables more iron. Lettuce and brassica crops formed firmer heads, and runner beans were stimulated to greater growth in mass.*

Requisite financial support from the Rudolf Steiner Scientific Research Fund in Stuttgart is gratefully acknowledged.

---

*These tests were made with the assistance of D. G. Remer.

Chapter Six

Feeding According to the Laws of Nature

Do We Feed Correctly?

On the whole, the production we demand of our domestic animals is unnatural. This cannot be fully compensated by better care and treatment, feeding and breeding[53]. The obvious weakening of the constitution of domestic animals is usually due to economic considerations. The farmer often keeps more animals than he can feed from his farm and consequently he buys in concentrates. These facilitate a quick capital turnover. But if they are given concentrates the animals will not make the best use of the coarser home-grown fodder, and also chronic diseases gradually creep in and their constitution deteriorates. The health of our stock is declining and is artificially supported by physio-chemistry, but the deterioration is noticeable in the quality of the animal products.

The quicker turnover achieved by this intensive animal husbandry is likely to be lost in the future through chronic diseases such as sterility, grass tetany (grass staggers), acetonaemia in cattle and muscular dystrophy, cough and oedemic diseases in pigs and other animals.

Infectious diseases can be treated successfully with antibiotics but the healing of a weakened constitution and diseases of the endocrine metabolism are among the most difficult tasks of therapy.

Since "the organism is the bio-chemical counter-picture

of the milieu"[54], the cause of the deterioration of the constitution must be sought in the feeding and manuring. As a result of present-day manuring, plants will suffer more and moire deficiencies[55].

On the other hand, a new method of feeding can so affect the soil via the quality of the dung, that it will lead to a wholly new outlook on manuring.

Importance of Crude Fibre

Among the basic foodstuffs, carbohydrates rather than fats and proteins are the most important energy-producing substances. But the readily digestible carbohydrates such as sugar and white flour are not the most suitable food for animals. On the contrary, coping with the less easily digested carbohydrates and crude fibre, which are richer in carbon and salts, calls forth forces which make the organism lively and vigorous.

	Carbon content, in %
Cellulose	44.4
Lignin	55–60
Cutin (in cell walls)	68–70
Sugar only	40

The digestion of the less digestible carbohydrates and crude fibre is set in motion by the cholinergic nervous system. Through the sympathetic nervous system the whole organism is challenged to develop its own forces[56] for improving assimilation. When feeding sugar, quite different processes take place via the adrenal vegetative activity of the sympathetic system. Adrenalin becomes active, and this encourages catabolic processes. The organism is only temporarily satisfied and is over-stimulated.

Although the carbon chain compounds in crude fibre

and sugar are closely related, their action is quite different. Crude fibre is not a clearly defined chemical concept. It comprises the insoluble remains of a plant after boiling for 30 minutes in 1.25% sulphuric acid, 30 minutes in 1.25% potassium hydroxide, and then washing in water, alcohol and ether.

	Fibre content in %
Rye chaff . . .	43
Linseed chaff . . .	30
Rye straw . . .	40
Good hay . . .	26
Bad hay . . .	30
Dried Jerusalem artichoke haulm	23
Lucerne hay in flower . . .	30
Cocksfoot straw . . .	40
Dry potato flakes . . .	22
Oats . . .	9
Barley . . .	5

The use that animals make of fibre can vary greatly. Sugar however is quickly assimilated. Cows do not tolerate it very well because of the fermentation it causes in the rumen. But horses and pigs can be fed sugar. The horseman Captain Paul Bausil and his stallion Midas became famous. In a long-distance ride of 210 km—Paris, Rouen, Deauville—he arrived first, with the fastest time and a dry horse—no sweating. He had got his horse into condition by regular work, gradually increasing the sugar intake so that it could assimilate 3 kg of sugar per day in water[57]. But the feeding of sugar in the long term is detrimental, as has been seen when sugar beet growers have fed molasses to their horses. The horses became flabby, sickness-prone and sweated easily, which is always a sign of weakness and lack of endurance.

Crude Fibre, A New Discovery

Kellner's feeding experiments with steers showed a lower weight increase when their feed was supplemented with straw containing 40% crude fibre. It was deduced from this that the straw required additional work from the animals and thus more calories. Consequently, to this day it is thought that less easily digestible roughage is not suitable for the required high productivity of farm animals[58]. Similar experiments today would show the same results if the animals have not been conditioned to consuming roughage by careful management.

Captain Bausil had to condition his famous stallion. It took him weeks to get his horse into the condition in which it could assimilate such a quantity of sugar. How much more would this be necessary with crude fibre!

Eventually in 1935 Barboriak's experiments with rabbits[59] contradicted Kellner's idea. When his rabbits were given 60 g wheat straw per animal per day in addition to their normal rations, they showed a marked daily weight increase. The teeth and caecum of the rabbit are adapted to cope with fibre, as are the teeth and rumen of the ruminant. The rabbit's intestine is 5.6 m long and five days are required before defaecation is completed[60]. The caecum of hares and rabbits has a much greater diameter than any other part of the intestine and the greatest capacity. It serves for the digestion of fibre, as can be seen from its contents. The faeces from the caecum contain more protein than the rest of the droppings. The former contain 39.5% crude protein as against 13.8% in the latter, and less crude fibre, only 19.5% as against 39.1%. The caecum pellets are a little darker and smaller than the others. Through bacterial activity vitamins of the B complex are formed during the digestion of the fibre. All rodents utilise these by eating their own caecum droppings. (In children who eat their excrement it is a sign that they have not yet found their own identity. In rodents it has become a physiological necessity.) Rabbits become stunted if they are deprived of their caecum droppings unless they get some green fodder. Mice die after a few days if they do not get their caecum droppings. This was probably why the mouse of von Trenk[61], once of European fame, died after it was taken away from the unfortunate prisoner. On his request, the mouse which he had trained was not killed but presented to the wife of the commandant, in a cage. This obviously prevented it from eating its droppings and it soon died.

Crude Fibre and Poultry, Roughage and Pigs

The digestion in the two caeca of hens (birds have two caeca) is of equal importance for the breakdown of crude fibre and the provision of vitamins. The contents of the caecum have more crude fibre, niacin, pantothenic acid, folic acid and biotin than the rest of the gut content. The vitamins have a close relationship to the utilisation of food and the internal respiratory processes. Deprived of its caeca a hen's intestinal activity is altered and the excrement becomes watery[62]. This leads to the putrefaction of protein in the intestine and parasitic infections. Crude fibre is generally rich in minerals such as calcium and silica. The hen needs both: calcium for the eggshell, silica for its feathers. Feathers contain 1–2% of silica.

The great importance of intestinal bacteria has also been confirmed in pigs. If pigs are given raw potatoes and the rest of the food contains no vitamins of the B complex[63] they are nevertheless in the best of health. With boiled potatoes in similar circumstances, health and growth suffer. Raw potatoes stimulate the multiplication of *Clostridium butyricum*, and bacteria which produce biotin, paraminobenzoic acid and the necessary B vitamins. This does not mean that we should feed pigs on raw potatoes. It is merely an indication of how the less easily digestible foods or roughage stimulate a useful intestinal flora. Putrefaction in the intestine can be overcome in this way; chaff for example is particularly good for breeding sows.

In the Homburg Children's Hospital[64] babies fed with semolina were less affected with rickets and rachitic tetany than those fed on oat gruel. Every mother knows that oats facilitate the digestion and make the stool easier to pass, whereas semolina makes it firmer. So oats and wheat have different actions. An apparent vitamin deficiency can be caused mainly by the diet and does not necessarily indicate absence of the vitamins. The intake of supplementary vitamins can have very bad results. Vitamin D for instance can lead to the hypercalcaemia syndrome (raised calcium level in the blood and arterial sclerosis).

Cattle, the Best Utilisers of Roughage and Crude Fibre

Cattle are masters in developing and controlling their intestinal population for the digestion of fibre. The rumen, with a capacity of 120–150 litres, harbours 15 to 20 species of micro-fauna. These take part in the breakdown of cellulose and multiply in the rumen and are consumed in the abomasum. One cubic centimeter of the content of the rumen contains approximately one million such organisms. They are very sensitive to copper sulphate. The micro-flora population is far greater. One cc of the rumen content contains thirty thousand million very interesting micro-organisms. It is calculated that there are about 400 g of them in the rumen which are constantly multiplying and are consumed in the abomasum. There are protein builders and destroyers, cellulose consumers, producers of vitamins, synthesisers of acids, in short, specialists in every direction. The acidity in the rumen is between pH 2.8 and 4.1, the water content 85%. In the reticulum a new stage of digestion begins. The water content is reduced to 50–65%, the acidity is lowered and in the abomasum everything becomes liquid again as a slightly acid chyle. The contents of the intestine are alkaline and neutral. A new microbial flora appears; 47.5% are streptococci and 21.5% are coliform bacteria[65].

pH values in the intestine[66]						
	Abomasum	Duodenum	Jejunum	Illeum	Caecum	Colon	Rectum
Cattle	4.9–5.5	5.9–6.8	8.5	7.9	9.41	-	7.1
Horses	4.4	7.1–7.5	7.4–7.8	-	7.2	6.9–7.1	6.24

The well-regulated work of the intestinal flora enables ruminants to manage on cheap roughage between lactations or in winter and at times of food shortage. On a farm north of Berlin, owing to lack of hay, the cows were fed for many weeks on barley straw and water. They gave 7–10 litres of milk without losing condition, because they had been accustomed to cheap roughage. The average yield per cow is low, but the fodder is very cheap, though the cow must always have an adequate quantity. This means 5 tonnes of dry matter per year for a cow weighing 500 kg. Cattle are able to adjust their own organism, as well as their intestinal population, to their fodder. This can lead to extraordinary extremes. Just as they can utilise straw, so can they utilise fish meal instead of soya meal. Sheep in Iceland often have to eat dried fish as part of their winter ration. These are however cases of extreme necessity. Even more extreme is the feeding of urea. Today, as much as 1% is added to silage. All this simply shows the extraordinary wisdom in the organism of the cow and the adaptability of its metabolism, which can of course be greatly misused. But the organism needs time to adapt. This is why a change of fodder should be avoided if possible. A change of surroundings can also disturb the equilibrium of the organism and induce latent tendencies to illnesses.

When a farm is converted to a new system of management, especially under extreme soil conditions, hidden illnesses can emerge; but they will disappear when the new equilibrium has been found. As soon as the organism of the ruminant has adapted itself to the soil and its fodder plants, its production increases if the type of fodder is right. The cow, withdrawn into itself as it is, feels the inherent wisdom of the processes of the earthly metabolism out of which the plant world has arisen. As an example of the way that the ruminants develop their digestive organs from the fodder they eat, Hermann von Nathusius[67] quotes the famous English Shorthorn breeder Bates of Kirk Leavington who, as a result of his careful breeding policy was able to keep twice as many cattle on his farm as his successor. While in practice the standard food rations are often inadequate, there are many examples where the opposite is the case. It follows that the breeder has to select a type of animal which suits the home-grown fodder and the environment. It is therefore necessary to arrange a cycle of feeding and manuring which is not influenced by intake from outside and into which the organism of the cow can integrate. Changes in manuring can cause great disturbances. This was experienced by Australian sheep farmers during the Second World War. When they had to do without superphosphate, fertility of the ewes dropped to 10% in some cases. The fall in fertility was however not only a result of the lack of phosphate but also of the introduction of subterranean clover, the seed of which is reputed to encourage weight increase. This clover thrives on phosphate and made it possible to graze two to four times the number of sheep on the same acreage. When the phosphate was no longer available the clover developed oestrogens which influenced the metabolism of the sheep. (This can happen over here with the use of poultry manure and slurry.) The catastrophic infertility lasted for two years, 1941–1943, and Voisin said: "If the Australian farmer had been obliged to wait for the verdict of the biochemists, not many sheep would have remained in Western Australia"[68]. The promotion of subterranean clover did not prove of lasting value since it was dependent on excessive phosphates. (Only after ten years of chemical investigations was it discovered that a disturbance of the oestrogen metabolism had occurred.)

In this connection we can quote the experiences of some farmers in Eastern Germany from 1934 to 1937. As a result of Rudolf Steiner's lectures in Koberwitz, these farmers had introduced a self-contained cycle of feeding and manuring. After only one year, all the farms showed a better utilisation of fodder, and as a result, they could keep more animals. Harald Kabisch[69] described the same thing in the case of some Bavarian farmers in the years 1950 to 1964. Even prior to the Second World War it was found that, before conversion to the self-contained cycle, 100 kg starch equivalent produced 4 kg of butterfat and after conversion 7 kg.

In another case the butterfat rose from 7.49 to 10.50 kg[70]. This increase in yield is not a result of more concentrates, but on the contrary of a better utilisation of home-grown roughage in the cycle of the self-contained farm organism.

The enormous influence of grass on the development of the stomach of ruminants was demonstrated by Hermann von Nathusius in 1880 in the case of two lambs. The one was reared on milk only and the other had milk and pasture. After 30 days the lambs were slaughtered and the volume of their stomachs compared.

Volume of	Milk fed lamb	Milk and pasture lamb
Rumen	372 ml	1832 ml
Omasum	19 ml	206 ml
Reticulum plus abomasum	640 ml	803 ml

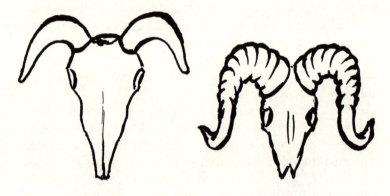

High quality food type
Negretti sheep

Roughage type
Indian mountain sheep

(Drawings by H. von Nathusius)

Roughage develops the digestive organs and glands. Too much protein-rich fodder overburdens the organism (particularly the liver) with toxic residues. This chemical stress can be more upsetting to the organism than the mechanical one of roughage. The organic unity of cattle, food plants and soil life is of more importance than the generally accepted requirements of protein, starch and certain minerals.

In this cycle phosphorus, potassium, etc. show a comparatively broad range of variation. Compared with human milk the chemical composition of normal cow's milk is subject to greater variation.

| | mg per litre[71] | |
	Human milk	Cow's milk
Potassium	37.5 - 63.5	38 - 287
Calcium	17.0 - 60.0	56 - 381
Phosphorus	6.3 - 26.8	56 - 112

These variations are due to fodder. If we look among the minerals for a standard of evaluation, our attention is drawn to the principle mineral in the roughage. This is silica. The silica content determines the quality of good roughage (See pages 43 to 45).

Cattle Thrive on Roughage

Cattle require 17 days for total defaecation, sheep 16 days[72]. If the feed is too rich in protein the toxic residues of protein breakdown exert a detrimental effect throughout this time. Roughage has the opposite effect. The forces of digestion are called upon and counteract the process of decay. Roughage retards, whereas concentrates accelerate digestion. Roughage suits the unhurried nature of the cow, while grain and concentrates, rich in protein, suit the bird nature, whose digestion takes but a few hours.

Coarse hay remained in the rumen of a camel 16 days and was only completely evacuated on the 22nd day. Most of it passed through in three days. A mixed feed with grain shortened this time. It took only 22 hours instead of 72 for the main portion to be defaecated[73]. Statistics tell us that it takes 18 hours for the cow, but there is no mention of under what conditions.

The cow, among all our domestic animals, utilises the fibre of roughage best, if it is properly reared and fed.

| | Utilisation of crude fibre (Kellner) | | |
	in pasture-grass	in lucerne	in flowering clover
Cattle	77%	44%	59%
Horses	40%	39%	47%
Pigs	20%	22%	24%

These figures are approximate.

In the last century, landowners in Brandenburg and Pomerania were in the habit of feeding finely-chopped twigs of broad-leaved trees to cattle and horses, knowing how healthy and economical such coarse roughage was. In northern France and Pomerania* they grew the protein and fibre-rich gorse *(Ulex europeus)* for this purpose. It was chaffed and crushed for fodder[74].

Practical experience has shown that, perhaps owing to presence of the bitter substances, bark activates the digestion in intestine and liver and thus allows cattle to protect themselves more readily from intestinal, stomach and liver parasites. Rowan berries are particularly good for the liver.

Medical uses of hedgerow plants	
Willow	against fever and plant poisons
Hazel	for fertility
Gaultheria	clears deposits
Guelder rose	assists pregnancy
Rowan	strengthens the liver
Alder buckthorn	laxative and blood purifying
Sloes and sour cherries	rejuvenating
Mulberry	promotes digestion
Birch	antisclerotic
Elder	blood purifying
Barberries	regulate kidney activity

*(also in Wales. Transl.)

All this adds a further reason for planting shelter belts around grazing areas. If cattle are to be upholders of soil fertility they should not be deprived of the plants that belong to their nature.

In the rich and varied man-made landscape with the domestic animals belonging to it, every organism should benefit. The principle of the farm as an organism takes precedence over the laws of optimal feeding with protein and starch.

Physiological Effects of Crude Fibre in Animal Evolution

The farm organism gives only a limited insight into the reciprocal relationship of plant and animal. A better insight can be obtained from the general evolutionary development on our Earth as evidenced by paleontological finds and also from its spiritual evolution according to *Occult Science - an Outline* by Rudolf Steiner[75]. We must learn to read in both.

In early times our Earth was overgrown with formless aquatic plants. This was followed by weakly-rooted and non-flowering plants in a mainly warm, swampy landscape: mosses (without roots), ferns, *Selaginella* and the now extinct *Sigillaria* (in the Coal Measures) with rhizome-like organs, which spread out like roots in the swamp.

Plant life was more parasitic and saprophytic, with internal respiratory organs, originally of an anaerobic nature[76].

Only with the solidification of the Earth and the separation of the Moon, did a change take place. Plants became land-plants. Their formerly mycotrophic, saprophytic existence became transformed into autotrophic growth. Rhizomes arched themselves up somewhat like the tremendous root "knees" of the swamp cypress *(Taxodium disti-*

chum). Trees appeared. The tree has created in its trunk its own living soil above the mineral earth, on which a multitude of plantlets grow in order to absorb the increasingly intense sunlight. The plant world of conifers, cycads and ginkgo trees formed the forests of the Trias and Jurassic periods.

The great saurians who grazed the gigantic swamp and water plants disappeared. Land animals, the predecessors of our mammals, took on the task of consuming the masses of plant carbon. Otherwise everything would have perished and rotted and mankind would not have been able to find conditions on the Earth under which it could exist. First there appeared the duckbilled platypus, still amphibious, as the first mammal with milk glands. They exude a thick, sticky milk from skin protuberances.

Parallel with the land mammals, water mammals developed: marine mammals, whales, dolphins, sirens, seals, walruses and the herds of seacows grazing sea grasses and algae (Steller's seacow, recorded in 1768, weighed 4 tons). On land, development progressed in great strides. In the Jurassic, sloth-like creatures appeared, feeding on wood and leaves. In the Trias came the marsupials, often also eating wood and leaves, among them the kangaroo, an animal of the scrub desert.

Subsequently rodents and the great Elephantidae (mammoths) appeared. Plant life progressed to the stage of leafy trees and provided palms, planes, laurels and many other leafy trees and bushes. The Indian elephant feeds almost exclusively on the twigs, bark and fruit of trees. Only out of necessity will it eat grass[77]. Elephants use their tusks very cleverly to bring down bushes and trees. Beavers and elephants are wood eaters in a great way. The beaver fells whole woods. He builds dams with wood and brush wood and constructs canals to transport the wood. His diet is also wood, as his droppings show.

The elephant makes clearings in the jungle where the grass can spread and in doing so, consumes large quantities of bushes and brushwood.

Finally, we get the solipeds, animals with single hooves: the horse, ass, zebra—animals with strongly developed limbs, creatures of the open spaces. The ruminants appear with their highly developed digestive system and begin the digestion of fibre in the rumen, whereas the horse only utilises the caecum and colon. All these families of animals developed through feeding on wood and leaves. The forerunners of the horse *(Hyracotherium)* in both the Old and the New World[78] were pure leaf-eaters and woodland dwellers until the mid-Tertiary. This is to be seen from their teeth which have low crowns devoid of cement. The whole world of large animals evolved their diverse body shapes and capabilities by feeding on fibrous fodder, on wood, leaves and hard stems.

The first ruminants are, to a great extent, wood and leaf eaters. The camel, the first to appear, lives on hard fodder. Its favourite food is *Alhagi camelorum*, a leguminous bush of the desert. The giraffe, the next ruminant, browses on trees up to 5 meters high. Antelopes, goats and some sheep are also wood and leaf browsers. Cattle are the first to turn more towards the ground and eat grass interspersed with legumes on open pasture land.

The innumerable species of aquatic plants which originally were non-flowering, and later showed separate development of the sexes, were followed by productive land grasses[79] with more highly developed bisexual flowers, and seeds. Meadow grasses spread under the hooves of the herds of bison in North America. *Aristida* grasses, as tall as a man, serve the African ruminants as basic fodder. The kaffir buffalo is equally at home in swampy thickets or woodland and lives on coarse fodder.

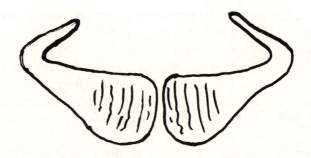

The strong horns of the African Buffalo

Sequence of Development

Plants
1. **Aquatic and swamp plants**
   Algae, fungi, ferns, equisetae, club mosses (Thallophytes)
2. **Land plants**
   Confiers, cycads, *Ginkgo*, *Araucaria*
   Broad-leaved trees: planes, palms, Lauraceae etc.
   Grasses and dicotyledons
   Leguminosae[81]

Animals
1. **Water animals[82]**
   Fish
   Saurians
2. **Land animals[83]**
   Duckbills are first sucklers with milk glands
   Marsupials
   Sloths, Megatherion
   Elephantidae, pig-like animals
   Odd-toed animals and even-toed ruminants:
   camels, giraffes, antelopes, goats, sheep and *cattle*

Reindeer, musk-ox, deer, roe deer and elk also like bushes and leaves. The musk-ox seeks out the dwarf willow in the far north. Elk eat the bark of broad-leaved trees and, to balance it, crop the water lilies in the freshwater lakes, just as rhinoceros eat lotus flowers.

Thus the rich succession of forms in the higher animals develops in conjunction with woody plants. They develop their strength and vitality from this type of plant so that they can survive as living conditions become harder, and at the same time they enhance the life of the soil through their digestive processes.

The crude fibre in wood and leaf shapes and develops the digestive system. The minerals in crude fibre—silica, calcium and potassium—lay the foundation for bones, nerves and blood.

The first Elephantidae (e.g. *Dinotherium giganteum*) could tear up rhizomes with their down-turned tusks. The later ones have upward-curving tusks by means of which they can break the bushes and trees they want to eat.

The highest stage of development in the large herbivorous animals is attained by the various races of cattle in both the Old and New Worlds. Cattle are the culmination of the hollow-horned animals which have a strongly developed frontal bone. This frontal bone, however, is not accompanied by the development of consciousness as in man; in fact, with its remarkable extension into the horns, it serves to turn the forces of the head back into the digestive system. A sort of spiritual brain forms in the metabolic system which, with great wisdom, controls and orders the upward regurgitation of the cud and its downward return.

The sequence of development is thought to be: camels, giraffes (with skin-covered projections from the frontal bone), antelopes (horns with solid core), goats, sheep, *cattle* (with true hollow spaces in the bony core inside the horn).

The "type" of the horned ruminant is not only governed by an inner directing principle, it does not merely obey the principle of its own nature[84] but it is also influenced by outer conditions. These very differing out conditions give rise to a diversity of forms which each have their special tasks serving the fertility of the earth.

Each individual is part of the whole process of evolution. The overall development is repeated in the single animal—in this case the development from the browsing to the grazing animal. Shrubs and grass in the right proportion provide the conditions that ruminants require.

This basic law of development overrides the laws of optimal requirements of protein and starch equivalents. This path should therefore be followed so as to avoid damaging he internal organs. Even a slight bodily weakness will certainly seriously harm the instinctive life and cause disturbances of the endocrine processes. Animal psychologists have known this for a long time but their work has been ignored in practical agriculture[85].

Importance of Subsidiary Substances—Resins, Fats, Oils and Tannin

It is not only hard woody substances that are taken in with leaves and twigs. Twigs and bark, leaves and conifer branches are rich in silica, calcium, phosphorus and potash. The foliage of trees and bushes in river valleys and meadows are usually so rich in potash that the grazing animals seek the sodium of salt-containing soils to balance it. In addition, the woody plants contain bitter principles, tannic acids, resins, fats and essential oils. These help ruminants to digest crude fibre more easily.

The cineol and phellandrene present in eucalyptus, which are related to caraway and peppermint oil, enable the koala bear (an Australian marsupial) to control its temperature. It is thus able to bear the extremes of temperature of the Australian bush[86].

We find something similar in our sheep. Shepherds like to take their sheep in Winter to places where they can find freshly felled conifer tops. The sheep will go out of their way to eat them. The needles of the tops are greener and richer in essential oils than those of the lower branches.

The resins, tannins and essential oils are supplemented in pastures by the labiates and umbellifers such as caraway, parsnip, burnet saxifrage, angelica and carrot. Ruminants make use of these substances to deal with their bulky plant diet rather as we take oil and vinegar with green salads. Animals can protect themselves from intestinal parasites by eating these sub stances, just as the tree protects itself against parasites with its resin. The connection of the bark beetle with the development of resin is well known; this in its turn depends on the substances the tree finds in the soil. Similar processes can be found in other circumstances[87].

Ruminants grow strong on coarse plant fodder and develop an astonishing ability to utilise roughage so that they can maintain their native physical strength, endurance and health.

For cattle, the change-over to concentrated feed causes far-reaching changes in the glands of the digestive system and in the protein-forming organs, heart, lungs, liver and kidneys. The normal pulse rate of cattle is 40 to 50 beats a minute. Following systematic conversion to concentrate feeding, cows of the Kostroma breed of horned cattle on the Karayevo collective farm in the (former) USSR had a pulse rate of 70 to 86 beats and a respiratory rate of 40 to 44 breaths per minutes instead of the normal 12 to 25. The blood pressure of the young cattle from 1–1/2 to 2 years was the same as that of adult cattle. The inner organs,

Running Reindeer in Lapland

In 1911 there were still 30 million caribou in Canada, in 1938 only 2.5
million. The caribou or wild reindeer was the basic food of the North
American Indians and the Eskimos.

heart, liver, kidneys and spleen, weighed 1.5 to twice as
much as those of normal cattle. The milk yield of the large
herds exceeded 6000 kg per cow per year[88]. This is the
result of the rigid application of the Darwinian evolutionary theory of adaptation and development which ignores
the natural characteristics of the "type". As a result of the
world economic situation (transport and world trade) excellent financial gains can be achieved by feeding concentrates, but in the end a breakdown of health will show
that this policy does not pay.

The dung of intensively fed animals poses new problems and leads to incorrect and undesirable decomposition
processes. The cow becomes a bad servant of soil fertility.

On farms in Poland where cattle were fed on ensiled sugarbeet pulp and vinasse* and a high ration of concentrates, continual decalcification of the soil was observed although hardly any nitrogenous fertiliser was used.

On the other hand, ruminants can make the soil rich and fertile with their dung and urine. The prairies and grassland of the savannas, so rich in humus, have arisen in this way and thus provide mankind with the conditions necessary for the cultivation of food crops. It was the large mammals which made the Earth fertile for mankind. But in the last 150 years something like 60% of the humus layer, so painstakingly built up through millenia, has been lost to humanity by desertification and general wastage.

Nevertheless, the animal as a helper is not yet lost to us! But it must be restored to health again. Through digesting large quantities of roughage strong bones will develop to serve as a foundation for the nervous system. Teeth, horn and antlers are encouraged in the *fore part* of the animal, while the *digestive system* promotes fertility, longevity, productivity and good utilisation of fodder.

Even India, in spite of its reverence for the cow, has lost the knowledge of this fundamental fact. The Indian people have the greatest number of cows in the world. It is estimated that in 1960 there were about 175 million cattle (excluding water buffalo). Comparable figures for West Germany were 12 million and for the USA about 90 million. But the severe lack of food for the cattle and the burning of dung as fuel turn cattle into destroyers of the landscape in India. Otherwise the cow dung could easily provide the basis for producing enough food for 400 million people.

---

*A by-product of sugar beet processing.

89

Leaves and Straw as a Source of Minerals

There is wide-spread concern about mineral deficiencies. We have rickets, osteoporosis, loss of condition in Winter, diarrhoea, milk fever, grass tetany, acetonaemia, puerperal convulsions, prolapse, parasite infection, sterility etc[89]. The usual deficiencies are in calcium and phosphorus. Nowadays a calcium-phosphorus ratio of 1:1 to 2:1 is the aim. Deficiencies in the fodder and overstraining of the productive capacity of the organism through excessive protein feeding are responsible for the fact that far more disorders and illnesses appear today than formerly (See also p. 69 et seq.).

Hedges of leafy trees and bushes can be very valuable. Nevertheless, it is not wise to let cows that are already sick eat bark rich in tannic acid. The leaves of hazel, alder, lime and sycamore maple contain 2 to 3% lime and 0.6 to 0.8% phosphoric acid in the dry matter and have a protein content of 12.5 to 18.7%—far more than fodder grasses. The minerals in the green leaves are in a living condition, strongly influenced by light, and are very readily utilised by the animal organism. For a similar reason conifer woods are interplanted with broad-leaved trees which improve the litter layer and the development of the soil. Also in the prairies and savannas, woody shrubs have made these lands suitable for the large mammals.

The greatest population of bison lived formerly to the west of the Missouri rather than the Mississippi, though they were generally widespread throughout North America. The original population was estimated at about 60 million head[90]. From the Missouri to the mountains the land is too dry for wheat. To the east there is more rainfall and regular rotation is possible. However, the bison particularly likes the dry land and throve on the uneroded soil rich in lime and phosphorus[91]. The woody bushes contributed much to the neutrality of the soil and to its lime and phosphorus content and hence to the great number of bison.

Hedges not only contribute to active mineral processes. What they provide also stimulates glandular functions which detoxify the body. Instinct leads the sick animal to particular plants.

An outstanding example of the roughage type, a Heidschnucke ram

On the Luneburg Heath there are still 43 flocks comprising some 13,000 head of this breed. They represent the extreme roughage type among sheep and produce the very finest meat.

In the case of milk fever for instance, the parathyroid gland, which secretes parathyroid hormone[92] is thought to be partly responsible. Parathyroid hormone mobilises the calcium in the bones through its production of citric acid. Consequently the calcium level in the blood rises and the calcium content of the colostrum is increased. If however the parathyroid gland does not function, the familiar symptoms appear which today are more and more difficult for cows to overcome*[93].

Cattle are of a phlegmatic temperament, as every motorist who meets them on the road will know. Their feeling life tends to be inwardly absorbed in the liquefying processes of digestion and to be closely connected with it. Outwardly this appears as a sort of "resignation" and what one might call their dejected expression. Any stressful experience (as happens in cases of protein poisoning) can cause collapse[94].

Irregularities of pulse and respiration are often to be found, as well as faintness, convulsions (eclampsia) in the fore or hind parts of the animal. This may be associated with grass tetany or milk fever. Calcium, magnesium and boron can bring the animal round. In other cases the rhythm can be restored with strong coffee or with homoeopathic preparations of nux vomica, mercury, thornapple, *colchicum* or snake venum[95]. These are remedies suited to the bovine animal. For the horse—an animal of melancholy type—other homoeopathic remedies are more suitable: *Belladonna*, *Rhus toxicodendron* or formica. The sanguine temperament of the pig introduces a cheerful element. Its life processes, connected with light, encourage quick growth and the putting on of fat. Its animal nature is easily startled, for it is not deeply incarnated. Its life functions are very sensitive to outside stimuli. In the pig we have the "type" of the cheerful animal surrounded by its "heavenly" fat. When it is ill, its life body "crumbles"[96]. Erysipelas, which involves a breakdown of the

---

*The parathyroid gland also affects the silica level of the blood.

Rye and vetches on drained
marshland without manure

Manure treated with the bio-
dynamic preparations has a
particular effect on legumes

Rye and vetches on drained
marshland with B.D. composted
manure (10 tonnes per ha)

Shifting sand dunes as a result of neglected care of humus
(Fürstenwalde, Spree)

Rich fungal growth on a manure heap treated with the combined preparation.

Soil profile of podsol with a hard pan. Bleached sand horizon clearly visible below the top layer

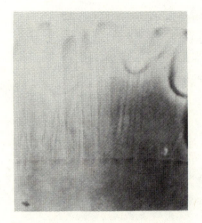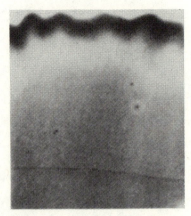

Chromatograph comparison of carrot juice
(a) Juice from carrots sprayed several times with silica preparation 501, potentised to D7
(b) Juice from untreated carrots

Chromatograph comparison of red cabbage juice
(a) Juice from red cabbage sprayed several times with silica preparation 501, potentised to D7
(b) Juice from untreated red cabbage

life-organisation, appears as patches of red rash on the skin. It is likely to be fatal.

The digestion of the pig can be supported by preparations of sulphur, silica, garlic and calcium. Nettles are particularly valuable for pigs, owing to their richness in lime, potash and silica on the one hand and iron for the blood on the other. Pigs should also get some roughage. Besides nettles, pigs can have chaff from oats and barley, the hard stalks of clover and serradella and even twigs from hedgerow shrubs. Pigs are very partial to twigs if they can get them.

Leaves and Trace Elements

Navel ill, which is often fatal in calves, is considered to be due to lack of trace elements, these include iron, copper, nickel, cobalt, manganese and molybdenum.

The colostrum of the mothers of dead calves have shown the following deficiencies:

Trace elements in the colostrum of cows[97], in mg/kg				
	Fe	Ni	Co	Mo
With healthy calves	15.36 ± 11.5	120 ± 19	2.14 ± 0.36	72 ± 14
with dead calves	2.18 ± 0.8	84 ± 4	1.61 ± 0.06	32 ± 4

The new-born calf normally brings a reserve of iron and copper with it for the production of blood before a new supply of these elements is taken in with plant food. If this is lacking the calves become anaemic and piglets have a crisis occurring in the third week. This can be overcome in piglets (to say cured is too much) by giving 2 to 3 ml orally of a solution of 10 g iron acetate, 1 g copper sulphate, 0.1 g cobalt nitrate per litre. Without copper the iron deficiency cannot be corrected. This also applies to sheep and cattle, which have far more copper in their livers than other mammals, including man[98].

	Copper content in the liver, in mg/kg dry matter
Man	24.9
Cattle	77.0 (200 according to Underwood)
Sheep	236.6 (up to 599 according to Underwood)
Horse	14.8
Pig	41.3
Dog	98.2
Rabbit	9.2

In this case species of broad-leaved trees are recommended as liver remedies. Ash, elder, alder, oak, birch and maple contain 11 to 18 mg of copper per kg dry matter. Grasses contain only about half as much. Even clover, which is comparatively rich in copper, does not attain these levels[99].

Intensive high-protein feeds, on the other hand, attack the stable protein structure of the glands, which consequently fail to function. The animal cannot overcome and eliminate the poisons in the food. If food is inadequately digested and not transformed, but enters directly as untransformed substance into the body, the result is illness and death. The activity of the glands and their capacity to secrete need to be stimulated. Wood and bark heighten the development of this inner activity of secretion.

A comparison of the copper content of leaves and grasses clearly shows that here we have an organic remedy for the copper deficiency discovered by Voisin.

Copper content in mg/kg dry matter in leaves and grass	
Sycamore maple (nitrogen accumulator)	7.7
Field maple	11.2
Birch	12.2
Oak	12.0
Alder (nitrogen accumulator)	13.6
Elder	12.0
Ash	18.2
Smooth oat grass	3.6
Cocksfoot	6.7
Crushed barley	2.7

The Use of Crude Fibre

If, in the Hippocratic sense, mankind is the measure of all things, this provides a key to the animal kingdom.

The human being develops in three seven-year periods until maturity. From birth until the seventh year—no longer dependent on the maternal organism—he should establish his own life functions: breathing, maintaining warmth, nutrition, secretion, growth and preparing the second teeth.

Then, until the 14th year, the feeling and emotional life grows to be an independent part of his organism. Thus the organism reaches a new level. In the body the bones continue to develop, the permanent teeth appear, digestion and secretion increase and puberty is reached.

These phases occur also in the animal, but they are compressed in time and mainly serve the needs of the body. In the case of cattle, the first phase has already reached a certain stage at the age of 6 to 9 months. They are then weaned and it can be seen from the teeth that a change is taking place.

Dentition of Cattle	
Age	4th pair of permanent molars
6–9 months	
18–21 months	1st pair of permanent incisors and
	5th pair of permanent molars
2 years	6th pair of permanent molars
2 years 6 months	2nd pair of permanent incisors and
	1st and 2nd pair permanent molars
3 years 6 months	3rd pair of permanent incisors and
	3rd pair permanent molars
4–5 years	4th pair of permanent incisors

(As the numbering of the molars appears confusing in the original, we have substituted the usual English and American numbering. Trans.)

From 18 months on there is a stronger growth of the horns as a metamorphosis of the upper corner incisors. The predominance of head forces produces teeth in cattle. The predominance of digestive forces produces sexuality. With hens we find a similar polarity between plumage growth and egg production. The animal has a continuous development of the teeth (as seen in rodents), but in man, owing to the development of intelligence, the teeth are subject to a retrogressive process, once they are formed. Consequently the animal can chew fodder better than man. Bone and antler formation is dependent on light as well. Good antlers only develop after a Winter of sufficient sunlight (cosmic nutrition)[100].

After 6 to 9 months the protein-rich food should be followed by a diet with plenty of roughage. Long hay (rich in silica), straw, a little oats in the sheaf, chaff, as well as soaked awns should be fed. This lays the foundation for bones, nerves, skin and membranes. The ability of the animal to utilise the plant world to the full is only attained on the development of the last (corner) incisors in the 4th to 5th years. Unfortunately today high yields are expected from the cow at an earlier age.

Heritable characteristics such as good fodder utilisation, butter fat and the ability to put on flesh, can only be developed before the age of sexual maturity 18–21 months. Good use should therefore be made of this period. Once the astral body (carrier of feeling and emotional life) is fully developed, it is too late. It is during this early period that the animal must be "educated" to utilise its fodder.

In order to accustom young stock to roughage and straw, they should only be housed in an open shed. In the open air their inner activity is enhanced. The animals soon learn to consume large quantities of straw and even rye straw in Winter. In warm housing, this does not happen. Feeding according to the need of the species should be combined with the provision of a natural life.

If they are fed in the right way in this early period, cattle can utilise large quantities of cheap roughage later on, as long as this meets their protein requirements. When in full milk, cattle need 12% crude protein in their fodder, less when they are dry. But sugar and flour are not suitable food for cows. They do more harm than good.

We need to learn anew to appreciate roughage and fibre as cattle-feed. They are cheaper to produce and suitable plants yield large quantities. The food of dairy cattle should have a 25% content of crude fibre. In the rumen, through fermentation, crude fibre stimulates the production of acetic acid and short-chain organic acids required for the synthesis of fats[101].

The principal bulk fodder plants today are maize for silage and roots, but they do not provide the best food. In the physiology of nutrition maize is known for its lack of tryptophan which is the basis for niacin formation. Roots indeed yield a large bulk of fodder but they and their leaves are unbalanced as regards mineral content. If the tall fodder grasses were subjected to equally intensive cultivation and manuring, the end product would be better. It is possible to achieve up to 15 tonnes of plant dry matter per hectare with the plants listed below. This is sufficient food for three adult cattle for a year.

High-yielding bulk fodder plants
1. Sorghum, fodder millet 3.50 m high
2. Jerusalem artichokes 3.50 m high
3. Timothy two to three cuts a year
4. *phalaris tuberosa,* a species of reed grass
5. Meadow fescue and tall fescue
6. Comfrey (for silage)
7. Lucerne (alfalfa)

In addition there should be regular availability of hedges round the grazing fields, both leys and permanent pasture.

This would constitute sensible continuation and enhancement of animal husbandry as formerly practiced in Europe, integrated into the landscape of forest and meadow. Cattle, horses and sheep either lived on forest grazings near the edges of the forest, or were kept in broad water meadows or river valleys with their hedges (still sometimes to be found in the district of Verden-an-der-Aller and Weser), or within the village boundaries sheltered by hedges, in the foothills and mountains.*

Once we have grasped and appreciated the character of a landscape and the farm belonging to it, certain guidelines emerge for the breeding and keeping of cattle and warn us against falling into extremes of specialisation which only produce short-lived results. Attempts to breed either very early maturing animals on a high protein diet or only sturdy animals on high-fibre roughage, transgress the laws of the continuously interrelated processes between soil and plant life. Really good animals require a

---

*Hedges are still to be found in Great Britain (Trans.)

98

Outdoor shelter for young stock in Sweden

balance between these opposites. In order to build up their health and constitution in perfect harmony, cattle are dependent on a healthy, self-contained farm organism. Any manure brought in from outside should, if possible, go through a preparatory composting process, in order not to introduce a disturbing element.

Feeding, Manuring and Soil Husbandry

60 to 120 kg silica-turnover per ha per year as a foundation for dynamic productivity

Today, it is in the high mountains that the connection between shrubs, grass, cattle and soil-formation can best be seen.

In the mountain valley the farmstead is immediately surrounded by the arable fields and grass leys. Then comes the hillside, grazing land for the cattle, with hazel shrubs and willows—these are particularly valuable—together with scattered maple, beech, oak, alder, birch and ash. Then the forest approaches with its lightly shaded fringe of under-shrubs, for the animals' delectation. On such a farm the visitor may notice quite a different type of cow dung. The cowpats are well formed, covered with a shiny membrane and are odourless. If this manure is piled up, there is no mould and no bad smelling decomposition, but it gradually turns black.

In the soil this dung is not likely to decompose in the wrong way. It is readily taken up by soil organisms and transformed into humus. Earthworms are to be found under the cowpats up to an altitude of 2000 m, well above the tree line.

Food high in fibre produces a mild dung which is not so apt to putrefy as dung from intensive feeding of concentrates or even of young, lush grass, Putrefaction results in the production of ammonia which unfortunately displaces the valuable bases in the soil (Ca,Mg,K) and renders the humus colloids soluble. The dissolved humus substances drain away with the ground water. Calcium and iron compounds arrest this flow. For this reason the leaves of trees high in calcium (ash, maple, elder, beech) are particularly valuable in woodlands. If not enough iron and bases (Ca,Mg,K) are available, these humus substances sink to the lower levels which contain less oxygen, and there they form pans which are injurious to the roots. Nature provides many examples showing clearly that the quality of the dung has a profound influence on the fertility of the soil. The creation of the fertile soil of our Earth is closely connected with the mode of life of the larger animals. Artificial alterations in food supply lead inevitably to changes in soil fertility.

The characteristic attribute of the valuable roughage that contributes to mild dung is its silica content. Liebig had the idea that a key to soil fertility lay in the solubility of silica[102].

To produce soil, plants must first utilise warmth and light in order to build up their carbon structure. Silica is the mediator of the forces of light and warmth above the earth; and below the surface it assists the forces of dynamic fertility by combining with humus as humus silicate. But in order to do this, the silica must be continuously transformed by plant and animal, so as to lay it open to the influences of the world of forces. Without this cycle the formation of the black earths is inconceivable, and this appears more and more as the revelation of a cosmic-terrestrial secret. In our latitudes the cow helps towards this. In the roughage she consumes, she processes up to 200 g of silica daily. This amounts to 60 kg per year and 120 kg per hectare, assuming two adult animals per hectare. Every day 10 g of silica are completely dissolved by the cow[103] and excreted in the potassium-rich urine. The greater quantity passes through the intestines. The intestinal mucus is also involved. The conversion in the urine is very high compared to man. The human being excretes only 0.2 g daily in the urine. It is mainly in the brain that he converts silica for the development of consciousness and the capacity to form mental images. It enables him to be aware of himself as an ego. The cow does not achieve ego-consciousness in the brain. She occupies herself with the silica in the metabolism where she forms a sort of supersensible brain. This works as a wisdom-filled regulator of the whole process of nutrition. This leads to a sort of rudimentary "ego-presence" in the digestive region and a connection of the dung with ego-forces—just the opposite of man. Thus the silica which the human being needs in the brain, reveals itself as an organising element in the living cycle of animal-plant-soil.

For this purpose, however, the silica must be broken down somewhere so that it can become an agent for perceiving and fixing peripheral forces and substances—a gateway facilitating assimilation by the plant and thus rendering the soil dynamically productive. By composting the manure with the bio-dynamic preparations these processes of sensitising are strengthened, particularly with the help of the silica forces of the dandelion preparation, supported by the other preparations.

What Rudolf Steiner in his *Agriculture* course refers to as the general relationship of mammals with shrubs[104] (though less intimate than that of birds with conifers), is also an essential part of the self-contained farm individuality.

When the Connections are Broken. . . .

Pig farmers today complain that pigs suffer increasingly from muscular dystrophy. Naturally, this entails financial loss[105]. The disease is a sign of an organic weakness of the nervous system. "For what develops as muscle can only maintain its form because the nerves are its builders"[106].

Nerves are stimulated by the root nature. Sodium and phosphorus are active in their physiological processes. Root forces are to be found in many forms in the fibrous matter of plants, and to a certain extent their diverse forms are adapted to the individual species of animals. The pig is actually a particularly "intelligent" animal, owing to its sense of smell and hearing. It uses the forces of its head and its sense organs (smell and hearing) both outwardly and inwardly. These are stimulated by roots and fibre.

Animal paradise.

Natural pig-keeping in woodland (Worme 1965)

Unfortunately, crude fibre is to a great extent excluded from its diet because it is not a sufficiently productive fodder. Fattening with crude fibre takes longer and time costs money. For convenience of mechanical mucking out, often no straw is used for bedding. In many cases the pigs bite each other, cannibalism appears and is then considered a vice. What is then more logical than to give the restless pigs a tranquilliser in their food!

So—a sleeping pill, while mankind sleeps! A new system of feeding would go a long way towards healing the considerable damage done by modern manuring.

Humus and Environment

One of the most important qualities of a good soil is its absorption capacity. This is chiefly due to the presence of true humus, for which we have to thank the mammals. A good humus soil collects moisture. It absorbs dew, and with this dew other substances enter the soil. We must assume for instance that the plant covers its sulphur requirements from the air[107], but a good humus content in the soil also plays a part in this.

The following table shows the capacity of humus to collect dew in comparison with other soils[108].

1000 g on 50 sq. inches	Dew collection at 15 to 19°C, in g			
	in 12 hr.	in 24 hr.	in 48 hr.	in 72 hr.
Quartz sand	0	0	0	0
Clay	22	26	28	28
Loamy clay	25	30	34	35
Gley soil (waterlogged)	30	36	40	41
Shaly marl	24	29	32	33
Arable soil	16	22	23	23
Garden soil	35	45	50	52
Humus	80	97	110	120

So where there is no humus, this must first be created in order to have healthy conditions.

Silica per hectare per year, from roughage				
	yield tonnes/ha	kg in 1000 tonnes	Silica (SiO) kg/ha	Potash (K O) kg/ha
Best reclaimed coastal marsh grassland	18 t. hay	27.2	300–400	320
Other reclaimed coastal marsh grassland	12 t. hay	33.8	240–330	240
Good meadow	10 t. hay	27.2	180–230	180
Sour meadow	5 t. hay	13.8	70	45
Irrigated meadow	12 t. hay	6.9	80	400
Rye straw	6 t. straw	18.8	112	60
Wheat straw	7 t. straw	31.0	217	63
Carrots	70 t. roots		120	300
Comfrey (20% crude protein in the leaf)	15 t. hay	25.0	375	785
Jerusalem artichoke 3.5 m high	100 t. green		180	250
Phacelia (up to 7° of frost)	lime 4.5%		phosphate 1.11%	

Roughage requirements (110)			
per head of adult animals	hay	fodder straw	bedding straw
Cattle, 210 grazing days	1.6 t.	0.4 t.	1.5 t.
Draught horses, 210 grazing days	1.6 t.	0.4 t.	1.5 t.
Sheep (6 adult animals) 210 grazing days	1.0 t.	1.0 t.	1.5 t.
Horses, the whole year	1.75 t.		1.5 t.
Oxen, the whole year	1.75 t.		1.5 t.

Normally a cow eats only 48 kg of grass when grazing. The content of dry matter is therefore decisive.

Summary

1. The digestion of fibre engenders an intenstinal flora with the help of which important substances vital for the organism are produced. Formative forces are called forth by fibre and these find expression in bone structure, teeth and growth of horns and enable the animal to be more productive.

2. From the evolutionary processes in the plant and animal worlds it is apparent that the animal does not depend on protein alone but acquires formative forces from its consumption of crude fibre. The reciprocal connection between the animal and plant world in evolution acts in a formative and shaping way on the plants and animals themselves.

3. Revised feeding methods would affect the soil through the better quality of the dung[109]. Physiologically appropriate feeding improves the health of domestic animals and, through their dung, the health of the soil also. Any disorders that appear, such as plant diseases and trace element deficiencies, cure themselves.

Chapter Seven

Supplementary Feeding using the Light Forces in Flowers and Dried Herbs

Due to modern ley farming, innumerable herbs have disappeared from our grass fields. But it has been shown that our domestic animals respond, even more than humans, to the healing properties of herbs. In herds where foot-and-mouth disease had broken out, the cattle very quickly resumed normal feeding and milk production when treated with herb teas. Sowing herbs and clovers in grazing fields has proved very valuable. Wide experience has demonstrated how cattle relish an aromatic herbal brew* added to their fodder, and how it improves their condition and yield.

In the main, representatives of three plant families should be allowed a place in the herb garden for their medicinal qualities.

1. The Umbelliferae (carrot family)

They supply roots and seeds. The peculiarities of this family are apparent in the inter-penetration of root and flower processes. The roots are mostly aromatic and also coloured. They are tap roots, enlarged by the flower forces in them.

---

*This is made by pouring boiling water on a variety of dried herbs including nettles and hay seed, leaving it to cool and adding it to the feed.

On the other hand the principle of the tap root and stem works right into the inflorescence and the seeds. By the penetration of the root forces into the seeds these become oil-bearing and aromatic. The form-giving forces of the lower parts of the plants appear in the seeds as wings, prickles and strangely transformed outer coverings. The seeds take on an almost insect-like appearance. They have prickles and bands giving the impression of a chitin covering, and sometimes exude an almost animal smell. Half-ripe coriander seeds have a distinct smell of bugs.

It is known that dried roots act especially in the realm of the nerves and senses. Young stock benefit particularly from being fed on (fresh) carrots and parsnips—especially sheep. This gives alertness, quick reactions and well-formed growth because it opens the senses to the surroundings in which the animal lives. Mobility and good bone formation are visible results. The nerve-sense system is situated mainly in the head and spine, but naturally, it penetrates the whole body. In certain areas of the body the development of this system can be obstructed and congestions can occur but if the appropriate plants are found, it is possible to help the animal organism over such difficulties in its development.

Roots and their relationship to certain organs	
Carrots	nerves and bones
Parsnips	nerves
Angelica	respiratory organs and milk production
Masterwort	stomach
Lovage	Lower digestive tract
Parsley	kidneys
Celeriac	kidneys and reproductive system

The leaves of the Umbelliferae are valuable food supplements. Parsley in the Winter should always be available, also in the kitchen. Fresh dill is readily eaten. It regulates the rhythm of the digestive system, and is of great value for nervous disorders. The leaves of the Umbelliferae have an association with lactic acid fermentation. This is why dill is used in pickling gherkins. Caraway in silage has the same function and also in sour dough for bread making. The following leaves are a useful supplement to silage: caraway, dill, lovage, celeriac, angelica, parsley and chervil. The most important parts of the Umbelliferae are the seeds. They enable the nerve-sense system to work down into the digestive system properly. They are therefore much valued as bread seasoning. A recipe for bread making from the Pilatus monastery in the Black Forest contains the following seeds and roots: boiled celeriac, seeds of coriander, caraway, fennel, aniseed, the root of lovage (to counteract mould) and, from the gentian family, the common centaury. For the animals' herbal brew, the Umbelliferae seeds do not need to be ripe. The whole herb, exclusive of the root, is gathered before the seeds have ripened. It is then chopped and dried. Lovage and fennel are perennials; most of the others are biennials such as parsley, caraway and angelica. The Umbelliferae need a sunny position and should be rotated in beds.

2. The Labiatae (mint family)

The Labiatae or labiates may be called the real doctors of the plant world. They support the rhythmic system of the human being. In man it is the rhythmic system which keeps the organism healthy. When we observe the labiates, it is obvious that the lower stalk principle and the upper flower principle are completely integrated in the middle region of the plant. Neither root nor seed is used, but the dried leaf.

Nectar from labiates is medicine for bees. It is good to

plant these herbs in borders near the hives. A great number of the useful ones are perennial.

The essential oils of the labiates have a warming effect. Their pleasant and sometimes astringent aroma stimulates the sense of taste and thereby the activity of the glands. Thus they are eminently suitable as ingredients of the herbal brew for cattle. Individual species act either more on the lower or on the upper rhythmic system: lavender and rosemary particularly on the upper rhythmic system, lemon balm and marjoram on the lower.

The following labiates can be used as fodder supplements:

Sweet basil	(sown in the open)
Basil	(sown under glass)
Marjoram	(sown under glass)
Hyssop	(perennial)
Savory, summer	(annual)
Savory, winter	(perennial)
Thyme	(perennial)
Lemon balm	(perennial)
Bergamot	(perennial)
Peppermint	(perennial)
Sage	(perennial)

The perennial labiates are better supplied as plants. As dried herbs they can also be used as teas in the home.

3. The Compositae (daisy family)

The name refers to the enormous number of florets gathered together on a single receptacle. It also gives an indication of why it is essentially the flowers that are used as remedies. The flower process even penetrates the leaf system. Bitter substances arise in the leaf through the domination of the light-filled flower forces in the leaf system. These substances are sometimes so strong, for in-

110

stance in wormwood, tansy and pyrethrum, that an extract can poison insects.

As dried herbs they combat sepsis and inflammation in the digestive system. They have a cleansing effect on these organs.

The following can be used as dried leaves and when in flower:

Southernwood   (very important)
Rue   (in small quantities)
Mugwort
Wormwood   (only to use for indigestion)
Tarragon
Goldenrod
Tansy

All these plants are perennial.

Southernwood, tarragon, mugwort, yarrow (in flower) and goldenrod are particularly recommended for a herbal brew. Southernwood and tansy are an excellent and mild remedy for intestinal worms.

Tansy should be dried in bunches and added to horses' hay in winter. Hay from marshy and wet fields should have a little wormwood mixed in with it.

The Blessed thistle is one of the most valuable medicinal herbs for the lungs and whole respiratory system. It is an annual of tremendous growth.

Medicinally used dried flowers of the Compositae family:

Chamomile
Yarrow
Marigold *(Calendula)*
Dandelion
Arnica

Common daisy
Cornflower
Sunflower petals

In these flowers the sulphurous element appears in many forms. Dried and crushed petals of calendula used as a powder are very effective dusted on inflamed and suppurating wounds and as a drench for internal ulcers. Dried and crushed tansy flowers should be given against intestinal worms. Chamomile should also always be included.

A valuable addition to dried herbs are the yellow flowers of St. John's Wort, cowslips and birdsfoot trefoil. These were specially recommended by Rudolf Steiner to enliven the metabolism. A very stimulating and pleasant tasting tea can be made of them. For a stronger action on the metabolism, the onion family can be used—chives for cattle, garlic for pigs. Through the sulphur in their oil, members of the onion family have a strong impact on the metabolic processes. The onion is like a flower bud resting in the soil.

Chapter Eight

Dynamic Fertility in the Farm Individuality

A Sociological Idea

"While in the west the attitude is: 'The world is the world, you have to live in it, at most you can think about social utopias', in Central Europe the attitude is: 'Man must become man in order to achieve true humanity; then he will find the Earth'[111]".

In order to encourage a person to try and understand humanity in general and the Earth as the destiny of humanity in a way befitting modern times, Goethe developed for Europe the idea of the "pedagogical province". Today we could say that the farm individuality as a rural cultural centre is becoming a human requirement of our time, especially for young people.

This new impulse comes at a time when agricultural technology is paramount in the west, while in the east, collectivisation is building the human being into the machinery without any consideration for the individual person.

The destruction of the Earth during the last 100 years has assumed unprecedented proportions. Sixty percent of the great forests and the humus reserves of the Earth have been destroyed.* The future food supply of the world is being endangered by the shortage of humus and the drying out of continents. In 1947 UNO announced that in the

*Written in 1965

113

great continents the deserts are advancing about 50 km a year over a width of 1600 km[112].

The Diaphragm of the Earth

It should be possible to grow economically viable, genuine quality produce on a farm managed along new lines according to the laws of life. But the profit motive is not the right starting point.

Often today it is not possible to make a profit in ordinary farming, or even enough to pay wages. This discourages quality production.

The ideas proceeding from Koberwitz (where Rudolf Steiner gave his *Agriculture* course) are not rightly understood if it is thought that agriculture must be made profitable before a farm can be converted to the new system. However, in the course of 42 years of practical application, we have learnt that if you want to convert a farm, at least the soil must be in reasonably good condition. A healthy, fertile soil—we may call it the "diaphragm" of the Earth— is a prerequisite for the self-contained farm individuality. The fact that in the *Agriculture* course the fertile soil is compared to the diaphragm has a deep significance.

In the human body, the diaphragm occupies a prominent position in regulating the breathing and the digestion. It is more developed in man than in the higher mammals. It is a very special sort of organ, an organ *sui generis*. In mammals it is not so fully developed, in birds even less so, and fishes, lizards and amphibians to not possess one at all.

The Greeks believed that the diaphragm was the seat of the soul, which lived in the breath. The diaphragm divides the upper from the lower man—the conscious from the unconscious parts. Similarly the living humus layer divides the earthly from the super-earthly, divides

114

terrestrial from cosmic activities and transforms them into upward and downward movement. Humus inhibits the direct penetration of cosmic forces into the plant. The direct influences from above change to indirect ones from below, via colloidal humic silicates, silica and clay. These, working upwards, cause the plant to produce digestible food substances out of the harder terrestrial ones.

The humus layer is the skin of the Earth through which it breathes in and out. The flowering plants which spread over the Earth are absorbed into the living soil in Autumn. Root processes, which develop in grasses throughout the Winter, ray out into the cosmos in the flowering process in Summer. Soil rich in humus absorbs water from dew (see page 104) and gives off carbon dioxide for the growing plants.

In the growing plant, metabolic processes take place above the humus layer. In the human being this happens below the diaphragm. In Summer the metabolism of the Earth extends as far upward as the wind carries the pollen and scent of the flowers. Usually we only pay attention to what the plant finds in the soil. But the plant could not build up soil if it had no connection with the atmospheric strata and cosmic influences.

Zones above the Earth

The first zone above the surface of the Earth is the moisture-laden air, the atmosphere. This extends to approximately 10 km in the temperate regions and up to 20 km in the tropics. In these regions clouds develop up to 6000 m. It is here that the stratosphere starts. Cosmic radiation converts oxygen to ozone. Ozone absorbs the solar spectrum extremely strongly in the range of 2100 to 2900 Å. Maximum ozone is at a height of about 25 km. Further out, at about 50 km, the ozone breaks down again, thus releasing heat. Two molecules of O_3 change to three of O_2 plus heat. thus a maximum temperature occurs at a height of about 50 km[114].

At 90 km part of the oxygen breaks up into oxygen ions. At 200 km and over, nitrogen is also involved in this process. At these heights light flares up brightly, causing "deaeration"[115].

Beyond 250 km there are very strong cosmic radiations which could endanger the astronaut by altering chemical processes in his body fluids.

The cosmic effects increase at higher altitudes. The region beyond 500 km from the Earth, called the exosphere, has been extensively explored up to 8000 km; but considering that the distance of the Moon from the Earth at apogee is about 300,000 km, exact research into cosmic space does not extend very far. It is known, however, that hydrogen plays a major part at great distances and is characteristic of the Sun's corona, which has the greatest influences on life on Earth.

Contemporary research corroborates Rudolf Steiner's statement of 1922[116].

Zones with Relationship to the Plant

Effects that influence life

Chemical effects
Zone in which light comes about

Warmth Zone — dynamic / physical — Blossom | Leaf-Leaf | Root and Seed

Airy Element

Watery Element

Earthy Element

All these zones—in their own individual ways—affect the diaphragm of the Earth and its covering of plants. Besides the strong chemical effect of ultraviolet radiation, there are further radiations at these heights which are less active in the tropics than at the poles.

Life from the Periphery as a Source of Nutritive Substances

The development of the plant world is connected with these influences. In the flower, warmth processes meet the warmth of the cosmos. In the Araceae the temperature of the flower rises by 10–20°C[117]. The flowers of *Victoria regia* (Great water lily) are detectably warmer than their surroundings. In these large flowers this is easy to verify.

Parklike pasture in Dannwisch

117

In the leaf the plant is connected with the elements of air and water, and it takes *from the air* the greater part of its substance in the form of water, carbon dioxide and even nitrogen and sulphur to a certain extent (C,O,H,N,S). The influences that come to the Earth from the farthest distances are of the greatest significance for the formation of the roots and seeds of our cultivated plants.

Animals also have a connection with the cosmic surroundings and with light. An alternation of heat and cold makes pigs short and stocky. The excessive length of modern breeds could not be produced without the even temperature of warm pighouses[118]. These types, however, are rather prone to disease.

The effect of light has also been studied. Frogs possess the capacity to change colour according to the light. If the eyelids of experimental animals are sewn up, they do not change colour[119].

It has been found that with ducks different qualities of light affect the reproductive glands. Long-wave red light increases the size of the testicles of the drake[120].

Light has an influence on the antler formation of the stag and the roebuck. It is well known that every Winter, from November to March, the antlers are renewed. Apart from food, the number of hours of sunlight is the most important factor governing their growth[121].

The sensation of light is led from the eye to the thalamus and impulses from there proceed to th hypophysis (pituitary gland). Thus the sense organs are involved in the building up of the body. But for this to occur, the physical nutrition must activate a healthy inner life in nerves and senses.

In the same way the surrounding cosmos must awaken this activity in the humus layer of the Earth. Domestic animals contribute by their dung.

The cheapest sty is the healthiest
Pasture for weaners in Verlussmoor

Activating the Topsoil

The soil cannot be built up simply by incorporating organic substances because before long they are usually broken down by the soil organisms. The life of the soil is so many-sided and varied that its digestive capacity can adjust to and cope with any organic substance, even with

119

chemical compounds. Great changes can be brought about in the life of the soil by manuring and soil cultivation and these may threaten its structure and productive capacity[122]. This is the tragedy of modern agricultural practice which, with its large, heavy machines, often disturbs the continuity and dynamic of soil development.

A deficiency of humus in the diaphragm of the Earth and its rapid breakdown, have led to the use of bought-in materials such as organic refuse, feathers, wool and pig bristles which are pre-digested by composting, in order to build up the Earth's diaphragm with mature humus which promotes its receptivity to the influence of the environment.

Loss of Soil Nutrients and Building up the Soil with Organic Nitrogen

Every living organism is in some way connected with its environment. In the soil, the soil fauna, fungi, algae and bacteria are all working together to form the so-called edaphon or soil community. In essence, this constitutes a single large organism of protein. Its principal constituent is living, active nitrogen. The versatile and varied living forms of nitrogen receive the most diverse cosmic influences. Hence nitrogen is a carrier of life. This is why nitrogenous manuring produces such successful results. But because all mineral forms of nitrogen lead to multiple disturbances of the continuity between soil layers (displacement of the bases Ca and Mg and of metals such as Cu)[123], a biological method of introducing the nitrogen should be found. Liebig said of nitrogenous mineral fertiliser that it is profitable only to the renter of the land (not the owner).[124] Even if organic nitrogen does not produce such a high yield, nevertheless for the private landowner, and also from the point of view of the national economy, it would be better to build up the soil to make it more productive for the future. Besides this, providing the soil with organic nitrogen would greatly reduce the need for all the other plant nutrients, because nitrogen *salts* increase the leaching of these nutrients.

In Holstein and Bavaria the annual loss of lime through leaching was 500 kg/ha in 1966[125]. Today it is considered necessary to lime the soil heavily with 25 to 50 tonnes per ha. But this can result in displacement of potash, sodium, boron and copper[126]. Of course, nitrogen has a crucial role to play in agriculture. ("Ponder the 'what' but ponder more the 'how'", *Faust, part II*, Goethe).

However, it is not so simple to build up the soil with organic matter. The organic substances can all too easily be completely decomposed. This can even result in the production of root poisons and injurious humic acids. The life of the soil can adapt itself to whatever is given to it. It adapts itself instantly; but it is not always beneficial, if the soil life changes.

In earlier times manurial substances were sought from other regions of the earth, i.e. a horizontal movement of materials was sought rather than a vertical connection with the atmosphere. Even in Liebig's day there was a dispute over the cosmic and the earthly relationships of nitrogen. Liebig did not wish artificial nitrogen to be introduced into the soil, but he was faced with the problem of replacing potash and phosphorus. His opponents held that artificial nitrogen was the most important thing for successful results. Liebig had recommended building factories to produce potash and phosphorus. These however went bankrupt because no results were obtained from these fertilizers, which were like rock dust composed of burnt and ground minerals, containing insoluble potash and phosphates. But to the end of his life, Liebig persistently maintained that artificial nitrogen was wrong and

121

dangerous for the soil. However, his greatest opponent, for instance Wolff in Hohenheim, and Lawes and Gilchrist in England, had great success with the use of artificial nitrogen.

This conflict in classical agriculture continues today. Every opinion may be right in some respects. In one respect the representatives of the nitrogen theory were right. Nitrogen brings life in its wake and conveys it to the soil and it is the most effective means of production in agriculture. The question is, in what form to use it.

The humus in the diaphragm of the Earth must be built up from organic manure, either home produced or bought in, so that the enlivened soil can itself take in nitrogen and transform this nitrogen from the air into protein. The legume family plays a great part in this. It has been found that with a certain mixture of manure, grass sods and marl with the addition of the herbal preparations, rhizobial composts can be made, which stimulate the growth of legumes[127]. We can learn to "milk" the legumes.

In this connection we should bear in mind lucerne. One hectare of lucerne can accumulate up to 300 kg of nitrogen in its green parts. This is the crude protein requirement for three head of cattle, and these will produce about 200 kg organic nitrogen in their dung and urine. Thus one hectare of lucerne can produce the organic nitrogen required for three hectares of arable land. This shows how much nitrogen lucerne produces in the form of protein, even without counting what comes from the roots. So far, there is hardly a plant known to agriculture that can equal this. Today, through breeding, careful planting and cultivation, there are many possibilities of growing lucerne even in the *lightest* soils, so long as the ground-water level is not too high.

A second plant which has the same yield but tolerates wetter conditions is Persian clover. This should be sown in Spring without a cover crop. Then it will give a similar yield to lucerne, besides being easier to establish.

In any case more use should be made of legumes. They have been much neglected owing to the mechanisation of cultivation and the use of the combine harvester.

After the First World War, Koch (Göttingen) found that manuring with sugar provided enormous possibilities of nitrogen production[128]. Of course, molasses cannot be used as a manure, owing to its high cost, but it is very interesting that it promotes the intensive production of nitrogen by the soil itself. Perhaps we should try to influence soil life in the direction of making the carbohydrates more soluble and thus encouraging a greater production of nitrogen[129]. The Nobel prize winner Virtanen showed that with red clover he could produce up to 500 kg nitrogen per hectare[130]. It has also been observed that soil algae can produce nitrogen[131]. Schanderl[132], working on nitrogen fixation by plants in pot experiments, established that a considerable build-up of nitrogen occurred even in non-leguminous plants, for instance in species of *Epilobium* (willowherb) and maple. In field trials it was observed that the build-up of nitrogen is much easier on clay soils than on sandy soils. Although the process is more difficult on sand, even there the manure can be used in such a way that the humus and nitrogen in the soil can be increased.

The nitrogen reserves of the soil must then be converted in part from a fixed form into a form that the plants can take up, especially into nitrate. This takes place at an optimal pH of 6.5 to 7.3 and in the living topsoil. If the soil is ploughed too deeply the conversion into nitrate cannot take place owing to lack of oxygen. In the deeper layers, ammonia is formed instead. Ammonia is a wonderful manure for fungi. If the diaphragm of the Earth is to be built up, the cultivation of the soil must be given careful thought.

A surprising result of nitrogen fixation appeared in France. In the south, in the Rhone delta, there is an infertile wet region known as the Camargue. The French wanted to grow rice there to supply the European market. The area was drained with due regard to irrigation. Algerian farmers were settled where formerly there had been shepherds and herdsmen. On cultivation, French scientists found that on this soil, up to 90 kg of nitrogen per hectare was produced in one week[133]. In a period when the soil is very active, the fixation of atmospheric nitrogen proceeds very rapidly. Of course we cannot simply extrapolate from this figure: one week at 90 kg x 52 in a year. There are times when the soil with its nitrogen behaves like bees with the honey harvest. Suddenly an unprecedented activity sets in, when a great deal of nitrogen from the world ocean of air is taken in and brought into the realm of the living.

The Role of the Sun

When the diaphragm of the Earth has been cultivated for a while, it becomes an active diaphragm. The farm begins to become an organism. This makes it possible for it to become self-contained to a certain degree. In many districts this is very difficult to achieve. Nevertheless it is very important for the farmer to strive towards this goal. Development in this direction depends on the fact that the Sun as well as the cosmos works on every single farm individually. The Sun influences every geographical part of the Earth in a different way.

There are creatures—the bees—which can tell us something about the effects of the Sun. They are pure Sun creatures. Sex plays but a very small part in their lives, and their social life is therefore all the more important. Bees work only for the community. They are very sensitive to light, having two enormous eyes as well as three small ones on their forehead. The various and multiple eyes indicate how strongly bees are connected with and dependent on the influences of the Sun. All their life rhythms are based upon Sun rhythms. When bees communicate information on newly discovered sources of honey through their "dance", they relate this to the position of the Sun, as von Frisch discovered.

Honey - Milk - Quartz

The communal life of the bee develops from its connection with Sun rhythms. Bees flying out in the world of nature are always seeking the Sun forces which are present in flowers as nectar. This nectar is actually the fluid quartz-principle of the soil, transformed and refined by the light which then becomes the pure rejuvenating force in honey. The fluid quartz-principle which the plants draw out of the soil—transformed, purified and rarified—is penetrated through with the hexagonal formative force of the Sun. The bees seek it out and live on it. Since honey transmits this form-building force, it is very important for man. Honey prevents brittleness and decalcification of the bones in elderly people. In order to avoid decalcification of the bones, and calcification of the arteries and brain, elderly people should eat honey. Honey makes people fine and lively. In earlier times, newly-weds were advised to eat honey so that their children would be beautiful and strong.

This quartz force is also present in milk. Where milk and honey flows, people thrive. This quartz force, this form-building force, comes from the Sun. The bees as social beings are in charge of it for the good of the land for which it is most important. Since the quartz force must be present in all plants, the continual transformation of quartz on the farm is very necessary. In modern agricultural practice no thought is given to the fact that quartz penetrates the plant sap and that thereby a corresponding light metabolism can take place. The silica content of plants is seldom the subject of experiments and therefore there are very few comparative analyses. But it is known that in the last 100 years it has greatly diminished.

	Wheat straw	Rye straw	Barley straw	Oat straw
Decrease of the silica content. From Duflas 1840[134] and Mentzel-Lengerke 1940[135]				
SiO$_2$ in the ash				
1840	81%	82%	71%	79%
1940	63%	48.2%	52%	46.5%

The quality of the straw has changed very much. This can be seen clearly in thatched roofs. Formerly they lasted 30 years, today at most 15 years.

It is not merely the quantity of silica in the plant, but the transformation of silica that is important. In cereals and grasses this is between approximately 200 and 400 kg per ha. Besides this there should also be a turnover of 10 kg of sodium, 80 kg of potassium, 40 kg of phosphate and 30 kg of calcium per hectare. This is easily achieved if the soil is in a living condition. Silica plays the most prominent and important role in furthering the influence of the Sun. This also applies to the animal world. Animals of the desert and steppes, such as antelopes, gazelles, springbocks and zebras are elegant and beautiful because the forming power of quartz works powerfully there through the Sun.

On the farm the Sun works not only directly but also

indirectly via quartz. This indirect effect of the Sun is especially important as the basis of formative forces.

For man too quartz, via the direct and indirect effect of the Sun in nature, plays a great part in the conscious and unconscious working of the ego. An example of this is the pancreas with its high silica content (5.2 mg per 100 g). Inadequate activity of the pancreas leads to diabetes. The malfunction of the peripheral circulation of diabetics shows that the ego-activity in the metabolism is disturbed. The silica content is very high in the human sense organs, where the ego is consciously in contact with the outer world. Silica is the element of the human ego-organisation and at the same time the element of the essence of the sun-light in agriculture. Every individual farm establishes a geographically distinct relationship with it, because the height of the Sun in the heavens and the length of day vary and therefore affect soil and plants differently.

Phosphorus and Sodium

A further connection of the Sun with life processes comes about because the Sun is a "giver of life". It is active wherever new life is created. In order that new life can arise, i.e. that life forces can become active, corresponding substances on the Earth must become mobile. Just as silica is necessary for the formative forces of the Sun to work, so earthly sodium and phosphorus from the surrounding universe must be available for the Sun's life-giving activity. Soda is sodium carbonate (Na_2CO_3). Sodium is a soft white metal. Wherever the action of light is required, as for the bleaching of laundry or tobacco, sodium is used as soda. The plant also needs sodium, where the influence of light is needed. Sodium is one of the bases involved in blood formation (Na, K, Ca, Mg). In the plant, sodium is present predominantly in the lower parts and also appears in the seeds. Phosphorus is active predominantly in the flower and the seed coat.

Percentage of phosphate (P_2O_5) in ash			
	Field beans	Vetches	Turnips
Seeds	39.5	37.2	47.7
Leaves	6.5	6.1	9.9
Percentage of Sodium (Na_2O) in ash			
	Chicory	Carrots	Turnips
Seeds	-	10	-
Leaves	8	6.5	3.9
Roots	15	15.8	5.7

Phosphorus appears in the seeds and especially in the seed coats. Birds eat the phosphorus-rich seeds. Bird droppings are the manure richest in phosphorus.

Phosphorus processes are initiated from above, sodium processes from below. The earthly sodium and heavenly phosphorus must meet in order that life may arise[136]. Wherever propagation and seed formation occur, sodium and phosphorus play a major part.

Earthly sodium and heavenly phosphorus must be properly directed if fertility in agriculture is to be maintained. It is because phosphorus and sodium are closely associated in the human brain that we can form thoughts[136]. This is spiritual fertility. The fertility which is of primary interest in agriculture works through the metabolism of the animal.

Phosphorus locked in the solid state appears in the bones, but its dynamic activity is in the nerves. They do not contain phosphorus in large amounts, but phosphorus-containing enzymes are present which continually set phosphorus free for the metabolism of the nerves. Sodium

128

Interaction of phosphorus and sodium[137]		
In prostate fluid, mg val/l		**In sperm, mg val/l**
Na	149 - 158	240 - 319
K	28 - 61	66 - 107
Ca	28 - 32	21 - 28
P	0.65 - 1.77	———

Phosphates (King-Armstrong units)
255–1727   500–4000
(mg val/l = milligram equivalent per litre)

Per 100 g of human brain	
Na	0.17
K	0.33
Ca	0.01
Mg	0.01
P	0.38

and phosphorus must be present in a certain ratio. Research into animal fertility has shown that the mineral metabolism of animals is no longer as it should be. This applies especially to potassium, calcium, magnesium, sodium and phosphorus. The sodium-phosphorus ratio is particularly seriously disturbed.

In agricultural husbandry the first consideration is cattle. In a very particular way cattle reflect sacred cosmic proportions. A twelfth of a cow's body is blood. She consumes an eighth of her body weight daily as fodder. Cattle connect their digestive processes with the Earth in a selfless manner, free of egoism, and thereby serve the Earth and bring cosmic order into the world of matter. Thus a cosmic fertilisation of the Earth takes place.

The composition of cow's milk is so remarkable that one single litre can supply a person's daily requirement of vitamins. On a healthy farm, when a cow is fed off half a hectare of land and yields 5000 litres of milk in the year, the quantity and ratio of phosphorus and sodium should correspond to that of the fodder plants. On a self-sufficient farm these relationships come into equilibrium and thus fertility is maintained.

Minerals per 5000 litres of cow's milk, in kg			
According to Geigy		According to Mentzel	
Sodium Na	3.5	Soda Na_2O	2–4
Potassium K	7.0	Potash K_2O	8.5
Phosphorus P	4.5	Phosphate P_2O_5	10
Calcium Ca	6.5	Lime CaO	8.5
		Nitrogen N	25

These minerals in the milk can be supplied by about half a hectare of fodder crops yielding 5 tonnes of dry matter. As regards sodium, some plants produce an excess and others are deficient.

Sodium content per 5 tonnes of dry matter, in kg			
Plants with an excess		Plants with a deficiency	
Barley and oat straw	13.0	Meadow hay	0.5 - 2.5
Lucerne	4.5	Ryegrass	0.7
White clover	26.0	Cocksfoot	0.7
Serradella	34.5	Yellow oatgrass	0.1
Stubble turnips	34.0	Red clover	0.3 - 2.5
Carrots	90.0	Turnips	3.7
Pasture	6.0	Rye straw	0.5

Many feed-stuffs do not meet the requisite sodium content and thus severe fertility problems can set in. Formerly the sodium content of plants was higher. Through man's interference with the soil as an organism, the content of silica and sodium in plants has seriously decreased.

130

In connection with this Andre Voisin wrote in *Grundgesetze der Dungung* Munich 1966, page 88:

The present standardisation of manuring in Europe will very soon lead to plant products which—in comparison with a century ago—will show changes in their organic composition, including the following:

Four times too much potassium
twice too much phosphorus
twice too little magnesium
six times too little sodium
three times too little copper etc.

It is obvious that such changes in the composition of our foodstuffs must have a very noticeable and lasting adverse effect upon human health, all the more, since these changes in the composition of plants also influence (though to a lesser degree) the composition of food of animal origin.

Decline of sodium content, in kg		
Per 5 tonnes of dry matter according to Mentzel (1940)		DLG, Table 25 (1960)
Barley straw	13.0	5.0
Oat straw	11.0	5.0 - 2.5
Rye straw	3.0	0.5
Wheat straw	2.0	0.5- 1.4
Potatoes	0.4	2.0
Fodder beet	3.0	5.0 - 30.0
Clover in flower	3.2	0.3 - 2.5
Lucerne in flower - Alfalfa	3.2	4.5
Meadow in flower	6.1	0.5 - 2.5
Pasture	-	6.0

Formerly barley was extremely rich in sodium. This has now changed. Barley is the cereal that grows furthest north and at the highest altitudes. It is able to do this because it still contains so much sodium, the earthly counterpart of light. Thus it requires a shorter period of growth and thrives in relatively low temperatures. Oats are similar. Barley straw and oat straw are such a valuable Winter fodder because they contain sodium. Lucerne, white clover, serradella and stubble turnips are outstandingly good fodder plants, owing to their high sodium content. But serradella and stubble turnips no longer have the same quality. Formerly stubble turnips grew very well in the Bremen district, even on deep sphagnum peat soils. But for the last 20 years they have no longer done well and cannot be grown on peatland soils. Can this perhaps be due to a sodium deficiency? Neither does serradella grow as well as formerly. No doubt, something has gone wrong. On good clay and reclaimed coastal marshland soils the sodium situation is better. This fact might give rise to the idea of applying sodium as a fertiliser. Luckily this is impossible for the soil would undergo saponification and become puddled and impermeable.

Since sodium-rich plants such as serradella and buckwheat no longer do well today, it is clear that something is out of order and disturbed in the soil balance of podsols, that there is a deficiency that lowers fertility. This could be cured by providing suitable living conditions for plants whose sodium activity would balance out these deficiencies; for instance certain legumes, carrots and stubble turnips. These plants also have curative value for cattle in Autumn and Winter. The treated animals get the sodium they require in Winter, and will not lose condition. Feeding carrots is a wise thing to do.

By means of the sodium-phosphorus function, the Sun creates ever new life and also stimulates the human brain to the creation of ever new thoughts. If the phosphorus-sodium interaction does not function properly in nature, reproduction processes in plants and animals become unsatisfactory. Also the resulting food used for human nutrition provides an insufficient basis for the development of thinking and consciousness. It is precisely through his consciousness that man is distinguished from the rest of nature. But as a result of the development of his consciousness he also has to assume a corresponding responsibility for nature.

Appropriate fodder plants must be found in order to create the right connection with the Sun. Animals quickly become accustomed to a feeding regime appropriate to their kind.

Instinctual Life in the Service of the Fertility of the Earth

There is still another relationship to the Sun apart from the geographical situation namely, that pertaining to hormone activity.

Psychologists refer to the Freudian theory that all emotion and behaviour are based on the sexual drive. Modern animal psychologists, have found through observation that, as well as the reproductive drive, animals have another instinct: the social instinct. This is predominant in bees for instance and can be observed in many other insects. Gosswald has described social behaviour in ants[138]. But it is also to be seen very clearly in some mammals, for instance beavers. These have two distinctly different phases in their behaviour[139]. In Spring they live in small family units, breed and then bring up their young. At the end of Summer they gather together in large groups in "village" communities. Then they reshape the landscape. They build dams of wood, filled in with mud to hold back water. They also construct channels in order to transport the wood. In this way the landscape of whole areas can be changed. The result is a great communal achievement, comparable to that of the Frieslanders who built the North Sea Dyke. This dyke is an even greater structure than the Great Wall of China. Similar constructions used to be built by the beavers of America, but the beavers have been almost exterminated. Today they are again being cared for and encouraged in order to conserve the water in the landscape.

A book on wolves by Lois Crisler described how a husband and wife observed the lives of wolves in Alaska. These two people believe they have found two different modes of behaviour in wolves. When the reproductive instinct is upon them, wolves will sometimes kill each other out of jealousy. Animals can be very jealous. If a person is in a field among horses and strokes one of them, all the others will gather round. If no notice is taken of them, they will nip the person. Elephants and tigers too can be jealous. At particular times animals can be unpredictable and dangerous. This is generally connected with the influence of the Winter Sun forces. Under the influence of the Summer Sun forces, when the beavers get their fat tails, they become very sociable. During the period when the social instinct prevails, wolves offer each other meat. They gulp down fresh meat and then regurgitate it to another wolf who has not had any. Orphaned whelps can be adopted, even dog puppies. Animals have a definite ritual in the communal life. We might call it the ritual of the social instinct.

Winter and Summer Sun affect the whole of nature—plants, animals and the soil fauna. Even domestic animals respond to the different influences throughout the year. The different influences of the Sun in Winter and Summer penetrate right into the metabolic activity of living creatures. It is known that different instincts and hormones develop in the different seasons. The hormones of the pituitary and adrenal cortex act in different ways on the distribution of soluble minerals in the body. For instance the parathyroid hormone of the parathyroid gland depends on the pituitary gland for its effect on the calcium and silica level in the blood. It has been shown that the emotional condition of a person alters his electrolyte balance. Through the use of radioactive tracers it has been found that the intercellular sodium and part of the fixed sodium in the bones increased noticeably during the psychotic period of depressions[140].

This completes the circle. The seasons of the year initiate the regulation of the electrolytes, the mineral salts, in the body. Animals make quite different use of a substance according to whether it is Summer or Winter. This varies with every part of the globe. Thus there is a certain adjustment and adaptation regarding minerals. Animals can be sparing or lavish with them, but this is not regulated by an ego as in man. This is the reason why cow's milk differs from human milk. Human milk has a fairly constant average content of potassium and sodium, while the potassium content of cow's milk can show a sevenfold variation. The human being has a constant rate of breathing: 72 breaths per minutes. In the case of animals the breathing adjusts itself and varies according to the way they are kept and fed.

An animal varies the quantities of mineral substances it secretes according to the message conveyed by its hormones. Some cows secrete three times as much calcium in their milk as others. During the first days after calving, one cow may lose 30 g of calcium per day in the colostrum, while another cow, with the same feeding, will lose only 10 g[141]. This has nothing to do with feeding, but is an inner disposition, which could have something to do with the time of year of its birth. This shows that an animal can adapt itself to a particular farm and the influences of its soil, climate and sunlight. A farm becomes self-contained through the adaptation of the animals to the fodder plants of a particular place. So we do not have to worry too much if there is not enough potash on our farm, as long as there are no symptoms of deficiency such as yellow and brown spots on the margins and tips of leaves[142]. An organism is able to accommodate itself to a certain extent to a higher or lower level, provided it is allowed to adjust itself smoothly, without disturbance. On some farms, although they are known to have a very low content of soluble potash, things grow well and the blood of the cows is particularly rich in magnesium. Grass tetany is unknown on these farms*.

Self-Healing and Resistance rather than Outside Help

Of course, a deficiency can lead to illness. But the first thing is to attempt to cure it within the self-contained entity of the farm itself. The totality of the farm should produce the solution, rather as today holistic medicine attempts to work out of a totality in the human being. For instance one could grow plants rich in potash; then soil and animal would mutually adapt to one another, resulting in an inner equilibrium where each keeps the other going. The dung thus produced would have a healing effect. Cow dung can cure many plant diseases. It is an exceptionally good remedy for clubroot (*Plasmodiophora*), take-all (*Ophiobolus graminis*), *Helminthosporium* and rust[143].

---

*Potash deficiency can be remedied with liquid manure, since animal urine usually contains 0.5% K_2O.

So cow dung is not only a manure, but can be a remedy for serious plant diseases or, better said, soil diseases. To achieve this requires the complete adaptation of the cattle to the actual land and its own fodder plants. A further result of this adaptation is a certain resistance of the animals to disease. In the desert, for instance, animals are extraordinarily disease resistant. In Africa a zebra was shot which appeared very fat and well nourished. On opening it up its stomach was found to be full of fat maggots *(Gastrophilus equi)*. A horse would have died of them. Possibly these fly larvae in the zebra were not only parasites but also assisted in the digestion of cellulose. Pests can also be useful if they are governed by the organism itself.

Animals can be attacked by many different sorts of parasites. This can be studied in the tropics. Rats living in natural surroundings do not have nearly so many parasites and are not nearly such dangerous disease-carriers as town rats[144]. Country rats are more disease resistant. The self-contained organism is the best guarantee of disease resistance in plants and animals.

The Human Being and the Farm Individuality

It is not enough to consider the farm individuality only from the scientific point of view. In science there are three methods of investigation. The first is the orthodox scientific method in which causes are investigated. The second is the organic method. Here we have to live with images of proportions and comparisons. The right numerical ratios for the health of the organism have to be ascertained, as has the amount a farm can sell and still remain healthy. This amount should only be one seventh part of its carbon production, perhaps about three to seven tonnes per hectare. In order to sell more, the turnover within the farm must be raised. For a farm to be considered as a "place in the realm of the Sun", the silica turnover should be about 120 to 150 kg per hectare per year. The fertile soils of the world have a nitrogen turnover of 60 kg per hectare per year. This quantity would be the standard nitrogen requirement (per three tonnes of carbon) for an individual self-contained farm. The minimum requirement of cattle would be 0.7 head of adult animals per hectare. Enough home-grown fodder should be produced for this minimum. The fundamental requirement is the controlled rotting of manure and composed materials for the "self-healing" of the soil.

Where these points are being adhered to, farm individuality is developing. Real nutritive quality will be produced.

But there is still a third method. The farm is more than merely an organism of plants and animals adapted to each other. It has become an individuality in its own right, a Sun-entity, an entity such as is to be found in man. Not a conscious one but rather, one with a dynamic potential. This entity, which is connected with the Sun, arises through the threefold action of the Sun. The *Agriculture* course contains a little sketch of this. It is a picture of a plant and above it is the whole influence of the ensouled landscape—a large red cloud. The plants are interconnected through the ensouled quality of the landscape. They constitute the organs of the soul of the Earth and below them is what humus brings to them as a gift from the cattle. This is the "ego-potential" of the farm individuality and is drawn as a chalice under the plant. On every farm it is something unique. It is not easy to describe. The scientific method cannot embrace it. Neither can the organic, quite. It can only be approached by what might be called a psychological-pneumatological method.

To summarise, we may say with Goethe: we cannot grasp and understand the spirit from how it *has* been and how it *has* acted, but only from how it *is* and how it *is* acting in this present moment[145].

The ego-potential which forms in the humus has a strong influence on the development of the soil. The effect of this individual and local collective influence of climate, soil, plant, animal and man is to be seen in the good utilisation of fodder by the domestic animal. In the herd this individuality is a quality which extends beyond the characteristics of the breed. An animal can be of good breeding and yet not adapt itself to become part of the farm individuality. It will not utilise its food so well. Hermann von Nathusius pointed this out in 1880[146]. A similar phenomenon appears in plants, as regards seed viability. Old gardeners knew that cow dung improves germination and viability in vegetables grown for seed. The vertical impulse of the plant pushes upward from the root, to connect the centre of the Earth with the Sun. The development of health, fertility and resistance in the plant is connected with the ego-potential in the manure. The plant can rise above the characteristics of the variety and can form populations tied to one specific farm, and even develop new heritable characteristics.

Besides the animal's utilisation of food and the viability of plant seed, the individuality of the whole farm shows itself in its basic productivity. On a self-sufficient farm every soil can be brought into a certain fundamental productivity[147]. This can be seen on many Swiss farms. This basic productivity can improve of its own accord, because well-tended soil can become more and more responsive due both to the direct and indirect influence of the Sun, and also to the continual supply of potash, phosphorus and sulphur via precipitation. The law of the individuality in agriculture applies all over the Earth, for the whole Earth is open to the influences of the Sun. The law of individuality also holds good for the Earth as a heavenly

The leader of the herd

The social element is to be seen in the order of precedence

body. From this law, individual, creative, fundamental basic productivity arises everywhere. Thus the farm can actually be compared with the human being. For the human being has something within him that unites him with all mankind regardless of race and blood relationship and at the same time is individual. In man, this realm is pure thought, arising from his ego. All human beings can meet each other in the realm of the mind. Agriculture is an area where the equivalent of this human capacity can be found in outer nature. Cultural life in the country involves bringing to life, caring for and managing this agricultural individuality, Without man, agriculture cannot exist. But as man cooperates with nature in building up this farm individuality he experiences the spiritual element in agriculture. There are of course machines on the land, but for this very reason the spirit in nature should be tended all the more, so that spirituality as a fructifying stream can flow back into mankind. The experience of consciously cultivating the spirituality in nature, can be for us an insight into the spiritual interrelationships of the world. The individuality of the farm on the one hand and the ego of man on the other hand make it possible for world-spirituality to enter the farm and for man to experience it.

Everything in farming follows the great rhythm of the Sun. A year, approximately 360 days, covers the normal food cycle on the farm. Seven years, 360 weeks, constitute a crop rotation. The life of a generation of forest is 360 years, and it takes seven times 360 years for the agricultural individuality to pass over into a new metamorphosis due to the movement of the stars. For this is the time required for the Sun at the vernal equinox to pass through one constellation of the zodiac. Bearing this in mind, farming is a great responsibility which cannot be carried by the farmer alone, but everyone should feel co-responsible for the land. The farm individuality calls for a social impulse among people who, in a practical way, are prepared to care for the spirit in nature.

The Independent Farmer, the Farm Individuality and Planned Economy

Experiences of a well known landowner of the planned economy of the First World War:

There are no two farms in Germany that are quite alike. Each one has its own peculiarities that only the farmer himself knows from long years of experience. But these are not known to the legislators, who can only make regulations to fit a farm that they have selected as typical. This lack of regard for the unique character of every farm must needs have detrimental effects on production. (Elard von Oldenburg-Januschau: *Erinnerungen*, Verlag Koehler und Amelang Leipzig, 1936, p. 148)

Nordic Sun-motif for religion and farming life.
Wooden church in Lapland with altar picture

Postscript

The husbanding of silica and carbon in all their forms gives a new direction to agricultural practice. Here we can only point to the first beginnings of a very necessary renewal of production methods. The trials which have been

142

described may serve to show how the new outlook can in practice lead to an increase in quality and fertility and later perhaps will stimulate future agricultural development. It has often happened that practice has preceded science. In our time this has often proved very fruitful. The individual practicing farmer makes no claim to a complete solution of all problems; he is a pioneer. Here I would like to thank all those farmers, far and near, who have contributed, and still do, to this very necessary on-going development.

Bibliography

1. *Steiner R.*, Agriculture. Lectures 7–16 June 1924.
2. *Rinteln*, Der Stickstoff, Düsseldorf 1961, p. 408.
3. *Kumada*, Humifizierung, Soil Science a. Plant. Nutr. *11*, 151, 1965.
4. *Hartmann*, Waldhumusdiagnose, Springer 1965, p. 38 et seq.
5. *Steiner R.*, Evolution of the Earth and Man. Lecture 10 9.9.1924. Anthroposophic Press, New York. 1987.
6. *Bergemann*, Das Mykorrhiza Problem, Allg. Forstzeitschr. 11, 1956, p. 297.
7. *Kaplan, W.*, Mutation als Motor der Evolution, Naturw. u. Medizin, 4, 1967, 71, Boehringer Mannheim.
8. *Tonzig, S., Bracci, Leda*, Nuovo Giorn. Bot. ital. N. 58, 1951, p. 258–270.
9. *Schanderl*, Botan. Bakteriologie, Stuttgart 1946.
10. *Müller, P.*, Nichtsymbiontische Fixierung von Luftstickstoff, Ber. Schweiz, Bot. Ges., 73, 1963, S. 347.
    Rauhe, Sitzg. Ber. Akad. Ldw. Berlin-Ost, XV H. 1. 1966.
11. *Remer, N.*, Güteerzeugung durch org. Düngung, Dem.-Post, 2, 1962.
12. *Waksman*, Soil Microbiology, New York 1952. *Krassilnikow, J.*, Berlin 1952.
13. *Pfeiffer, E.*, Amino acid. metabolism., Journ. of applied nutrition, 11, Nr. 319, 1958.
14. *Pfeiffer, E.*, A study of amino-acid metabolism with

urine, American review of tbc and pulm. Diseases, 76, Nr. 5, 1957.

15. *Müting,* Die Entgiftungsleistung der Leber (Glukuronsäuretest), Dt. Med. Wochenschr., 88, 130, 1963.
16. *Kaelin,* Hefte zue Erweiterung der Heilkunst, 3. Heft. Stuttgart 1953.
17. *Hegglin,* Differentialdiagnose innerer Krankheiten, 1961, p. 844.
18. Hdb. der Urologie, Göttingen, Heidelberg 1960.
19. *Weiss,* Diagnose und Prognose aus dem Harn, Ulm 1954.
20. *Richter,* *Völkenrode,* Praktische Viehfütterung, Stuttgart 1954.
21. *Klocke,* Berlin-Dahlem, Die Humusstoffe des Bodens als Wachstumsfaktoren, Parey, Berlin-Hamburg 1963.
22. *Rentschwik,* Arztl. Fortbildung, Genf, 9, 1963, p. 498.
23. *Fürst Pückler,* Andeutungen über Landschaftsgärtnerei, verbunden mit der Beschreibung ihrer praktischen Anwendung in Muskau, neu herausgeg. v. Deutschen Kunstverlag, Berlin 1933.
24. Dem. Mon. Schr., 12, 1937, p. 113.
25. *Scheiber, F.,* Bodenkundliche Bewirtschaftung von Talsandböden, Dis., Berlin 1931.
26. *Taderko,* Z. f. Pflzb. u. Bdkd., A. 12, p. 199, 1928.
27. *Remer, N.,* Dem. Mo. Schr., H. 7, 1937.
28. *Remer, N.,* Dem. Mo. Schr., p. 88, 1933.
29. *Garkuschka,* Bodenkunde, Bauernverlag Berlin 1953, Köhnlein, Z. f. Acker & Pflzb., Parey, Berlin, 122, 1965, 359.
30. *Remer, N.,* Bericht über Marienhöhe, Dem. Mo. Schr., 1936.
31. *Stellwag,* Kraut und Rüben, Müller, Planegg 1953.

32. *Duflos* und *Hirsch*, Oekonomische Chemie, Breslau 1842.

33. *Feldt, Hertsch, Wedell*, Pflzb., 7, 365, 1931.

34. *Lintzel*, Chemiker Z., 63, 1939, p. 226.

35. *Liebig, J. v.*, Theorie und Praxis, Braunschweig 1856.

36. *Niklewski*, Bdkd. u. Pflz. Ern., 49, 1937, 327.

37. *Remer, N.*, Der Kiesel und seine Bedeutung für die Landwirtschaft, Dem. Mon. Schr. 1933, p. 86, Bedeutung und Anwendung von Präparat 501, ebd. 1933, p. 97, Die Rindviehherde im Mittelpunkt eines Betriebsorganismus auf Sandböden, ebd. 1936, S. 171, Kiesel und Pflanzengesundheit, ebd. 1937, S. 75. Gesundheit und Leistung bei Haustieren, Planegg Münschen 1940.

38. *Tswett*, Die chromatographische Adsorbtionsanalyse Izd. An. SSSR. Moskau 1946.

39. *Kretowitsch*, Grundzüge der Biochemie der Pflanze, Jena 1965, p. 318, 335, 357 u. a.

40. The Morgan Soil-Testing-System Bull., 541, New Haven Connecticut, USA.

41. *Turba, F.*, Chromatographische Methoden in der Protein-Chemie, Springer, Jena 1954.

42. *Sinois*, Münch. Med. Wo. Schr., 106, 1964, p. 1180.

43. *Rein-Schneider*, Physiologie des Menschen, Springer, Berlin-Göttingen-Heidelberg 1960, p. 241.

44. Docum. Geigy, 6. Aufl., Basel 1960.

45. *Kretowitsch*, Grundzüge der Biochemie der Pflanze, Jena 1965, 8, 193, p. 116.

46. *Abrahamson* and *Widdowson*, Modern Dietary Treatment, London 1940, p. 334.

47. *Warburg*, Über den chemischen Mechanismus der Kohlensäureassimilation, Naturwissenschaften *43*, 1956, p. 237.

48. *Kretowitsch*, Grundzüge der Biochemie der Pflanze, Jena 1965.
49. Eisentest Merck, Ferropack Asal. Praecisions-Chemikalien, Wiesbaden.
50. *Lange*, Kolorim. Analyse, Verlag Chemie, Wiesbaden 1956, p. 463.
51. Futtertabelle der DLG, 1960.
52. Lebendige Erde, 1960, p. 88.
53. *Mayr, A.*, Zbl. f. Bakt., 191, H. 113, 1964, p. 37 u. f.
54. *Voisin, A.*, Boden und Pflanze, München 1959, p. 13.
55. *Voisin, A.*, Grundgesetze der Düngung, München 1966, p. 88.
56. *Carlson*, Biochemie, Stuttgart 1961, p. 281 und 310.
57. *Bausil, P.*, Paris-Rouen-Deauville, Mittler & Sohn, Berlin 1906.
58. *Kellner-Scheunert*, Grundzüge der Fütterungslehre, Berlin 1952, p. 201.
59. *Barboriak*, Diss., Zürich 1953.
60. *v. Buddenbrock*, Vergleichende Physiologie, Basel 1956, p. 343.
61. *Frh. v. Trenck*, Merkwürdige Lebensgeschichte, Reklam 3761/62.
62. *v. Buddenbrock*, p. 392.
63. *v. Buddenbrock*, p. 346.
64. *Hey* und *Schiefer*, Tagung der südd. Kinderârzte 21./22.5.1966, Alete Reihe 3/66, München, p. 38.
65. *Waksman*, Microbiol. antagonismen, New York 1945.
66. *v. Buddenbrock*, p. 340.
67. *Nathusius, II. v.*, Fragmente über Viehzucht, Paray, Berlin 1880, D. 64.
68. *Voisin, A.*, Boden und Pflanze, München 1959, p. 55.
69. Lebendige Erde, 1965, p. 6.
70. *Remer, N.*, Gesundheit und Leistung, Planegg b. München 1940.

71. Docum. Geigy, 6. Aufl., Basel 1960, unveränderter Nachdruck 1962, p. 484.
72. *v. Buddenbrock*, p. 343.
73. *Felaschini* und *Angelini*, Revista de Biologica 22, 637, 1937.
74. Dem. Mon. Schr. 1937, p. 123, P. v. Riepenhausen in Krangen, Privatdruck.
75. *Steiner, R.*, Occult Science, an outline. Rudolf Steiner Press, London 1963.
76. *Kretowitsch*, Grundzüge der Biochemie der Pflanze, Jena 1962.
77. *Zell*, Riesen der Tierwelt, Wien 1911, p. 346.
78. *Simpson*, Evolution des Pferdes, Naturw. u. Medizin 3, Nr. 14, Boehringer, Mannheim 1966.
79. *Hoogewerff, H.*, Spiegelung der Erdentwicklung im Pflanzenreich, Blätt. f. Anthr. *16*, 1964, p. 62.
80. Nach *Leunis*, Synopsis I, p. 246/247, Hannover 1887.
81. *Strassburger*, Lehrbuch der Botanik, Jena 1902.
82. *Leunis*, Synopsis der Tierkunde, Bd. 1, Hannover 1883, p. 656.
83. *Leunis*, Synopsis der Tierkunde, Bd. 1, Hannover 1883, p. 288ff.
84. *Steiner, R.*, Goethe the Scientist. Anthroposophic Press. New York 1950.
85. *Lorenz, C.*, Über tierisches und menschliches Verhalten, Bd. I, München 1965, p. 112.
86. *Krumbiegel*, Biologie der Säugetiere, Krefeld 1953.
87. *Wittich*, Der Stickstoff, Düsseldorf 1961, p. 367 u. a.
88. *Schaumjans*, Die Lage in der biologischen Wissenschaft, Moskau 1949, p. 317 D.
89. *Leroy-Delage*, Schriftenreihe über Mangelkrankheiten H 6, Stuttgart 1956.
90. *Heck, Lutz*, Tiere—mein Abenteuer, Wien 1952, S. 177.

91. *Nicol, H.*, Der Mensch und die Mikrobe, RoRoRo 1956.
92. *Ziegler, Lemmer, Minne, Pfeiffer, Heutsche*, Med. Wo. Schr., 91, 1966, 2114.
93. *Werr, J.*, Tierzucht und Tiermedizin, Stuttgart 1953.
94. *Warming*, Die Behandlung der Entzündung, Frankfurt 1947.
95. *Wolter, H.*, Klinische Homöopathie in der Veterinärmedizin, Ulm 1954.
96. *Werr, J.*, Tierzucht und Tiermedizin, Stuttgart 1953, S. 99.
97. *Leroy-Delage*, Schr. R. ü. Mangelkrankheiten, Kirchgessner H. 6, Stuttgart 1956, p. 76.
98. *v. Buddenbrock*, bergleichende Physiologie, Basel 1956, p. 596/597.
99. Arb. d. DLG, Bd. 62, Frankfurt 1960.
100. Prof. *Hollwich*, Med. Klinik 58, 1963.
101. *Haerkötter*, D. L. Pr. 89, 1966, 414 (H. gibt 15–20% Rohfaserbedarf im Futter an.) *Kirchgessner* und *Koch*, Der Tierzüchter, Hannover 13 1966, p. 452. Bei optimaler Fütterung von Rohfaser 18–22% in der Futterration lässt sich ein hoher Fettgehalt erzielen, Zucker und Stärke erniedrigen den Fettgehalt.
102. *Liebig, J. v.*, Theorie und Praxis, Braunschweig 1856, S. 101.
103. *Georgieff, R.*, Tierärztl. Mo. Schr., Bd. 44, Wien 1937, S. 78.
104. *Steiner, R.*, Agriculture. Lecture 7.
105. *Lannek*, Ätiol. Arpr. Prov. XVIII, World veterinary Congress, 1263, 1963.
106. *Steiner, R.*, Egyptian Myths and Mysteries. Lecture 7 p. 77. 1908. Anthroposophic Press, New York 1971.
107. *Schmalfuss, Z.* f. Pflz. Ern. Dg. Bkd., 1964, p. 116.
108. *Duflos* und *Hirsch*, Oekonomische Chemie, Breslau 1840.

109. *Voisin, A.*, Grundgesetze der Düngung, München 1964, p. 88.
110. *Hofmann*, Landw. Jb. 75, 1932, p. 951.
111. *Steiner, R.*, Eine Jahrhundertbetrachtung. Lecture 6.7.1923. A Review of the Century (English typescript only).
112. *St. Barbe-Baker*, Die grüne Herrlichkeit, Wiesbaden 1957, p. 207.
113. Wolkentafel für Wetterbeobachter auf See, Meterol. Amt, Hamburg 4.
114. *Schwentek, H.*, Max Plank Inst. Lindau, Die Lufthüllen der Erde und der Weltraum, Kempen, NDRH, 1959.
115. *Steiner, R.*, Spiritual Science and Medicine. Lectures 21.3. and 9.4. 1922. Rudolf Steiner Publishing Co. London 1948.
116. *Steiner, R.*, The Warmth Course. Lecture 14. 14.3.1920 Mercury Press. UA 1988.
117. *Strassburger*, Lehrb. f. Botanik, Jena 1902, p. 187.
118. Mitteilung von M. Rath, Farrach, Lavantal, Österreich.
119. *Stieglitz*, Z. f. vergl. Physiolog., 33, Berlin-Göttingen 1951, 99.
120. *Benoit*, Bull. Soc. Ophtalm. France 8, 1961, 835.
121. *Schumacher von Marienfrid, S.*, Jagd und Biol., Berlin 1939.
122. *Franz*, Z. f. Pflz. Ern. Dg. Bdk., 108, Wien 1965, 127.
123. *Nicol, H.*, Mensch und Mikrobe, RoRoRo, 1956, S. 119 (Basenverdrängung).
124. *Liebig, J. v.*, Theorie und Praxis, Braunschweig 1856, S. 53.
125. *Köhnlein*, Z. f. Acker u. Pflzb., 124, 1966, 212, u. Prof. *Schmidt-Mü.*, Vortrag in Giessen, 20. 10. 1966.
126. *Voisin, A.*, Grundgesetze der Düngung, München 1966, p. 61, 63, 75.

127. *Remer, N.,* D. L. Presse, 81, 1958, 447 u. Thornton & Meiklejohn, Ann. Review Mikrobiol., 11, 1957, 123.
128. *Koch,* Jahrb. DLG, 1918. Durch Zuckerdüngung wurden auf 1 ha umgerechnet 3200 kg N gebunden.
129. *Dahr,* Nitrogen Problem, 48. Indian Congress, Roorkee, 1961, p. 25. In mangelhafter Kohlehydratzufuhr liegt der Grund für den Verfall der Bodenfrucktbarkeit.
130. *Virtanen,* Nature, 138, 1936, 880 u. Suomen Kemisti, 10, 1937, 28.
131. *Waksman,* Soil Mikrobiol., New York 1952, p. 199.
132. *Schanderl,* Der Kartoffelbau, Nr. 1, Hildesheim 1961, S. 66.
133. *Rouquerol,* Anm. agron. (France), 15, 1964, 599. Die N-Fixierung der Böden belief sich bis 6 mg% Boden in 1 Woche.
134. *Duflos* und *Hirsch,* Oekonomische Chemie, Breslau 1840.
135. *Mentzel-Lengerke,* Landw. Kal., Parey, 1940.
136. *Steiner, R.,* Mensch und Welt. Lecture 3. 20.10.1923 The Essential Nature of Hydrogen. (English typescript only).
137. Docum. Geigy, Basel 1961.
138. Prof. *Gösswald,* Die kleine rote Waldameise, Metta-Kienau, Lüneburg 1952.
139. *Steiner, R.,* Health and Illness Vol. II Lecture, 10.1.1923, Anthroposophic Press, New York. 1983.
140. *Copp, A.,* Schan. D. M. Brit. med. J., 5370, 1963, 1439.
141. *Gomberg,* Hannover, Mitt. f. Tierärzte, Juni 1964, Trentschler, Laupheim.
142. *Hambridge, G.,* Amer. Soc. of Agron. and National Fertilizer Ass., Washington, 1941, (Hunger-Zeichen in Feldfrüchten).
143. *Bochow* und *Seidel,* Phytopathol. Z., 51, 1964, 291.

144. Ref. Therapie d. Gegenwart, 104, 1065, 1675 (Pestflohbefall der Ratten).
145. *Steiner, R.*, Truth and Knowledge. Bound with Philosophy of Spiritual Activity. Rudolf Steiner Publications. New York 1963.
146. *Nathusius, H. v.*, Vorträge Viehzucht und Rassenkenntnis, Berlin, Parey, 1890, p. 60, 139, 140, 107.
147. *Giesiger, Z.* Pflz. Ern. Dg. Bdk., 108, 1965, 161, "In der Schweiz gilt noch die Auffasung von Mitscherlich, dass gut mit K. u. P. versorgte Böden *ohne* die Zufuhr dieser Stoffe *bessere* Ernteergebnisse zeigen".

Glossary of Botanical Names of Plants, Grasses, Etc. Mentioned in the Text

Alder	*Alnus glutinasa*
Alder buckthorn	*Frangula alnus*
Angelica	*A. archangelica* or *Angelica sylvestris*
Aniseed	*Pimpinella anisum*
Arnica	*Arnica montana*
Ash	*Fraxinus excelsior*
Barberry	*Berberis* var.
Basil	*ocimum minimum*
Beech	*Fagus sylvatica*
Bergamot	*Monarda punctata* and *M. aurea*
Birch	*Betula* var.
Birdsfoot trefoil	*Lotus corniculata*
Buckwheat	*Fagopyrum esculentum*
Burnet saxifrage	*Pimpinella saxifraga*
Caraway	*Carum carvi*
Centaury	*Centaurium erythrea*
Chamomile	*Matricaria recutita*
Chervil	*Anthriscus cerefolium*
Chives	*Allium schoenoprasum*
Cocksfoot	*Dactylis glomerata*
Comfrey	*Symphytum officinale*

Coriander	*Coriandrum sativum*
Cornflower	*Centaurea cyanus*
Cowslip	*Primula veris*
Crimson clover	*Trifloium incarnatum*
Daisy	*Bellis perennis*
Dandelion	*Taraxicum officinale*
Dill	*Anethum graveolens*
Elder	*Sambucus niger*
Elder, red	*Sambucus racemosa*
Fennel	*Foeniculum vulgare*
Fescue, meadow	*Festuca pratensis*
Fescue, tall	*Festuca arundinacea*
Field maple	*Acer campestris*
Field pea (Peluschken)	*Pisum sativa*
Fir	*Abies alba*
Garlic	*Allium sativum*
Goldenrod	*Solidago virgaurea* and *S. Canadensis*
Gorse	*Ulex europeus*
Guelder rose	*Viburnum opulus*
Hazelnut	*Corylus avellana*
Hogs fennel	*Peucedanum ostruthium*
Hyssop	*Hyssopus officianlis*
Jerusalem artichoke	*Helianthus tuberosus*
Lavender	
Lemon balm	*Melissa officinalis*
Lovage	*Levisticum officinale*
Lucerne (alfalfa)	*Medicago sativa*

Marigold	*Calendula officinalis*
Marjoram	*Origanum vulgare*
Masterwort	*Peucedanum ostruthium*
Meadow fesue	*Festuca pratensis*
Meadow foxtail	*Alopecurus pratensis*
Mountain ash	*Sorbus aucuparia*
Mugwort	*Artemisia vulgaris*
Mulberry	*Morus niger*
Nettle	*Urtica dioica*
Norway spruce	*Picea abies*
Oak	*Quercus robur* or *Q. petraea*
Oatgrass, smooth	*Avenula pratensis*
Oatgrass, yellow	*Trisetum flavescens*
Parsley	*Petroselinum crispum*
Pelushken	*Pisum sativum*
Peppermint	*Mentha piperita*
Persian clover	*Trifolium resupinatum*
Phacelia	*Phacelia tanacetifolia*
Primrose	*Primula vulgaris*
Red clover	*Trifolium pratense*
Red elder	*Sambucus racemosa*
Red fescue	*Festuca rubra*
Reed grass sp.	*Phalaris tuberosa*
Rosemary	*Rosmarinus officinalis*
Rough meadow grass	*Poa trivialis*
Rowan	*Sorbus aucuparis*
Rue	*Ruta graveolens*
Rye grass	*Lolium perenne*

157

Sage	*Salvia officinalis*
St. John's Wort	*Hypericum* var.
St. Lucie's cherry	*Cerasus mahaleb*
Savory, Winter (per.)	*Satureja montana*
Savory, Summer (ann.)	*Satureja hortensis*
Seradella	*Ornithopus sativus*
Sloe	*Prunus spinosa*
Smooth oat grass	*Avenula pratensis*
Sour cherry	*Prunus avium*
Southernwood	*Artemisia abrotanum*
Spruce	*Picea abies*
Subterranean clover	*Trifolium subterraneum*
Sunflower	*Helianthus annus* and *H. rigidus*
Swamp cupress	*Taxodium distichum*
Sweet basil	*Ocimum basilicum*
Sycamore	*Acer pseudoplatanus*
Tall fescue	*Festuca arundinacea*
Tansy	*Tanactum vulgare*
Taragon	*Artemisia dracunculus*
Thyme	*Thymus* var.
Timothy	*Phleum pratense*
Willow	*Salix* var.
Willow herb	*Epilobium* var.
Wormwood	*Artemisia absintrium*
Yarrow	*Achillea millefolium*
Yellow oat grass	*Trisetum flavescens*
Yorkshire fog	*Holcus lanatus*